We know that your success goes beyond just the number on the scales; it's a combination of how you feel, your confidence, health and happiness (and so much more). That's why, whatever you want to do along with losing weight – eat healthier, be your best self, re-energise, de-stress or find fun ways to get moving, we'll give you everything you need to get there.

love food

Food is one of life's greatest joys. It nourishes us and keeps us strong. We don't believe in ever going hungry and we don't believe any food should be forbidden.

Eating healthier makes life better.
AND IT TASTES AMAZING.

WHAT'S *inside?*

HELLO
SmartPoints

SmartPoints is a simple counting system and it's really easy to use. It nudges you towards nutritious, healthier foods so that you eat better, feel better, have more energy and lose weight. **Now that's what we call smart**.

HERE'S HOW IT WORKS

Every food and drink has a SmartPoints value – one, easy-to-use number that's based on four components: calories, protein, sugar and saturated fat.

1 Calories establish the baseline of how many SmartPoints the food is worth.

2 Protein **lowers** the SmartPoints – more protein, fewer SmartPoints.

3 Sugar and saturated fat **increase** the SmartPoints.

> "YOU DON'T HAVE TO EAT LESS. YOU JUST HAVE TO EAT SMART."

 Personalise your food and activity plan to fit your life with a quick 2-minute quiz. Go to weightwatchers.com/uk to get started.

MOST FRUITS AND VEGETABLES ARE ZERO SMARTPOINTS. SO FILL UP ON THEM AND ENJOY.

You get a SmartPoints budget to spend on anything you like.
Stick to your budget and you'll lose weight. **It's that simple.**

Each day you have a
DAILY
SmartPoints
ALLOWANCE
which doesn't carry over, so use them or lose them.

Each week you have a
WEEKLY
SmartPoints
ALLOWANCE
to spend on splurges, bigger portions or going out.

You'll earn
FitPoints
for any activity you do.

If you're a nursing mum, have type 2 diabetes or are going through the menopause, see page 112. If you are a young person under 16, please speak to your Leader.

THE SCIENCE *bit*

SmartPoints works harder for you than simply counting calories. Calories don't tell the whole story. Neither do carbs or grams of fat.

Both of these choices below have the same calories, but common sense tells us that the ham thin and yogurt combo is clearly the healthier choice. With the SmartPoints system, the difference is clear.

This   *or this*

Jam doughnut. 250 calories.

Ham salad sandwich thin with fat-free yogurt. 250 calories.

And you can even add all of this for zero SmartPoints

SmartPoints is about more than just weight loss – it nudges you towards nutritious, healthier foods.

IT'S NOT CALLED *smart* FOR NOTHING.

2 ways TO FOLLOW SMARTPOINTS

Whichever you choose you'll lose weight eating delicious food that nourishes you from the inside out – and you can switch between them whenever you want. It's all about finding **what works best for you** today.

Count

You eat anything you like – nothing is off the menu.
Using a daily and weekly allowance gives you the freedom and flexibility to eat what you like and lose weight – nothing is off limits.

COUNT KNOW-HOW
ON PAGE 8

No Count

You get freedom from counting and tracking.
You focus your eating on a list of healthy foods and as long as you stick to these you don't have to count or track them. And you get a weekly allowance for anything that's not on the list.

NO COUNT KNOW-HOW
ON PAGE 11

Count KNOW-HOW

SPENDING YOUR SMARTPOINTS BUDGET

What should you eat and when should you eat it? The simple answer – it's totally up to you.

For most people, spreading their daily SmartPoints allowance through the day makes sense. You might want to spend more on dinner than breakfast or you may want to make sure you save some of your allowance for snacks. **It's all about making it work for you**.

Here's an example

(based on a SmartPoints allowance of 30)

Remember you've also got a weekly SmartPoints allowance to play with. You can use this any which way you like. Split them up over the week, save them all for the weekend or don't use them at all.

HOW DO I FIND SMARTPOINTS VALUES?

Right here

There's a handy basic list at the back
of this book for hundreds of the most
popular, everyday foods and drinks – see
page 103.

Online or Mobile*

Look up the SmartPoints for thousands
of everyday and branded foods, drinks
and restaurant meals and access our
SmartPoints calculator.

In Shop**

The directory for supermarket
shopping – SmartPoints for
thousands of foods and drinks
including your favourite
supermarkets and brands.

In Eat Out**

Get the inside track on eating
out with our genius guide –
SmartPoints for the menus of
your favourite restaurants.

* For Subscribers.
** Available to buy in your meeting or our online shop.

Here's how you could use the ideas in this book to spend your SmartPoints budget*:

BREAKFAST:

Banana honey overnight oats (page 35) .... **6** SmartPoints value

LUNCH:

Roasted butternut squash soup (page 59) .... **0** SmartPoints value

Turkey club on a bagel (page 50) .... **9** SmartPoints value

DINNER:

Quick beef bolognese (page 77) .... **3** SmartPoints value

60g wholewheat pasta .... **5** SmartPoints value

1 tbsp parmesan .... **2** SmartPoints value

SNACKS/EXTRAS:

¼ pint skimmed milk for tea/coffee throughout the day **2** SmartPoints value

Smart kale crisps (page 90) .... **1** SmartPoints value

Handful of blueberries and strawberries with
1 tbsp 0% fat Greek yogurt .... **1** SmartPoints value

Cheese triangle with grapes (page 89) .... **1** SmartPoints value

Add extra zero SmartPoints fruits and vegetables to your meals too –
but check the list of exceptions on page 109.

If you enjoy a glass of wine or some chocolate at the end of the
day, use your weekly SmartPoints allowance; don't deprive yourself,
have it, track it and enjoy it. 5 SmartPoints values will get you a
175ml glass medium white wine, and 2 squares of chocolate is 4
SmartPoints values.

* Based on a daily allowance of 30

No Count
KNOW-HOW

HOW DOES THIS WORK?

With the No Count approach, you focus your eating on a list of healthy foods and as long as you stick to these foods you don't have to weigh, measure or count them.

These foods come from **every food group** and you'll find that you have the basics in your cupboards and fridge already. The No Count list is on page 110.

You also get 2 tsp of healthy oil a day – olive, sunflower, safflower, rapeseed or flaxseed. You don't need to count the SmartPoints for these.

And with No Count, you have a weekly SmartPoints allowance which you can spend on foods that aren't on the No Count list – a glass of wine, a bag of crisps. It's your call.

The key to success with No Count is to listen to your body's hunger signals and to eat until you're satisfied – not stuffed, not starving – just comfortably full.

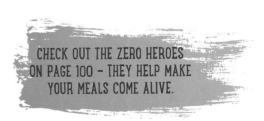

CHECK OUT THE ZERO HEROES
ON PAGE 100 – THEY HELP MAKE
YOUR MEALS COME ALIVE.

WHAT DO I EAT?

You choose! Eat whatever you like (from the list), whenever you like. No portion sizes to think about, just healthy, tasty foods to focus on. Eat portions that feel right for you. To build a meal, start with some lean protein and add a wholegrain and plenty of veggies or fruit.

It's easier to recognise how satisfied you are by eating less quickly and taking time to really enjoy your food. Don't let yourself get too hungry. If you're ravenous you're more likely to grab food – any food – and eat more of it than you need.

 If you track online or via your mobile app it's easy to use the No Count approach, simply choose it in your settings.

 Whenever you see this symbol, you're looking at a food, meal or recipe suitable for No Count.

THE NO COUNT FOOD LIST IS ON PAGE 110

Here's how you could use the ideas in this book to plan your eating on a No Count day:

BREAKFAST:
2 shredded wheat, ¼ pint skimmed milk and a sliced banana (page 33)

LUNCH:
Ham and tomato omelette (page 46)

0 SmartPoints salad with cheats vinaigrette (page 45)

0% fat Greek yogurt with mixed berries

DINNER:
Tandoori chicken with spiced yogurt (page 63)

Brown rice

Sweet meringues, Eton Mess (page 94)

SNACKS/EXTRAS:
Vegetable crudités with low fat cottage cheese

1 Weight Watchers in meeting chocolate bar

Add extra fruits and vegetables to your meals and snacks – check the No Count list on page 110 for what's included.

smart tips
AND TRICKS

KEEPING *track*

Fact: tracking what you eat helps you lose weight. It makes you aware of what you're eating, and how much you're eating. And it helps you stick to your SmartPoints budget. It's one of the most effective tools for successful weight loss.

But we're quite relaxed round here and for us, **tracking is not about being perfect, it's about doing the best you can**. If you're not sure how many SmartPoints are in that sandwich, a rough estimate is good enough for us. And if you're too busy to track today, why not take a photo of what you're eating so you can work out the SmartPoints another time.

○ You don't have to track any foods from the No Count list, but you do need to keep track of your weekly SmartPoints allowance.

DO IT YOUR WAY

Pen & paper?

Pick up a handy paper tracker at your meeting each week.

Something more gorgeous?

My Journal* is the place to write your very own success story – your 10-week diary for planning, tracking and celebrating.

Attached to your phone?

Our mobile app** puts quick and easy tracking at your fingertips.

Stuck on your screen?

Weight Watchers® online** does everything our mobile app does.

 Got a question about tracking? Get the answer 24/7 with Expert Chat on the Weight Watchers app or online at weightwatchers.com/uk

*Available to buy in your meeting or our online shop.
** For Subscribers.

SMART *planning*

Relying on willpower is a high-risk strategy – being prepared is so much easier (and much more effective). By planning your meals ahead, you can replace chaos with structure so that you don't have to make spur of the moment eating decisions, which often turn out to be high SmartPoints choices.

If planning 3 meals a day for a week seems too daunting a task, start by planning out just 1 meal each day. And if you want to leave room for spontaneity, then just plan 5 days and free-wheel on the other 2. The important thing is that you stick to your SmartPoints budget between weigh-ins.

TOP TIPS:

- Most of us tend to eat the same breakfasts – day in, day out. So start there – it means you can fill in 7 sections of your planner without too much thought.
- Look for opportunities to make the most of the ingredients you already have in your fridge and cupboards.
- Cook once, eat twice. We're big fans of batch cooking – it saves energy and time. The roasted vegetables you have for dinner today can be folded into tomorrow's lunchtime omelette.

FIND WHAT WORKS FOR YOU

A scrap of paper & a pen:

That's all it takes – 7 rows for the days, 3 columns for the meals!

My Journal*:

Your 10 week success diary for planning, tracking and staying in control.

*Available to buy in your meeting or our online shop.

My plan

FOR MY FIRST WEEK

DAY	BREAKFAST	LUNCH	DINNER
1			
2			
3			
4			
5			
6			
7			

SMART *shopping*

Put 'make a shopping list' at the very top of your 'to do' list!
A smart shopping list is possibly the most important thing
you can do to support your weight loss.

WE'VE GOT A GREAT BASIC SHOPPING LIST FOR YOU HERE:

PRODUCE
- ◯ Fresh fruit
- ◯ Fresh veg
- ◯ Fresh herbs and spices
- ◯ Prepared veg
- ◯ Potatoes
  (including sweet potatoes)

MEAT/POULTRY/FISH/ MEAT-FREE
- ◯ Skinless chicken/turkey breast
- ◯ Extra lean chicken/turkey/
  beef mince
- ◯ Lean beef steak
- ◯ Wafer thin chicken/ham
- ◯ White fish – cod/haddock/coley
- ◯ Bacon medallions
- ◯ Prawns

- ○ Salmon fillet
- ○ Tuna steak
- ○ Quorn mince
- ○ Quorn fillets/pieces

DAIRY

- ○ 0% fat natural Greek yogurt
- ○ Fat free plain natural yogurt
- ○ Skimmed milk
- ○ Low fat spread
- ○ Light feta cheese
- ○ Quark
- ○ Weight Watchers yogurt
- ○ Reduced fat cottage cheese
- ○ Low fat fromage frais

BREAD

- ○ Weight Watchers bread
- ○ Brown sandwich thins
- ○ Wholemeal wraps
- ○ Crumpets

CEREAL

- ○ Porridge oats
- ○ Wheat biscuits
  (like Weetabix)
- ○ Wheat cereal
  (like Shredded Wheat)

GRAINS/PASTA

- ○ Wholewheat pasta
- ○ Brown rice
- ○ Bulgur, quinoa, barley
- ○ Dry lentils

CANNED/CUPBOARD FOODS

- ○ Tinned tomatoes
- ○ Tomato purée
- ○ Chickpeas
- ○ Baked beans
- ○ Kidney beans
- ○ Canned fruit in juice
- ○ Canned veg in unsalted water
- ○ Tuna or salmon in water
- ○ Honey
- ○ Wholegrain mustard
- ○ Dijon mustard
- ○ Plain flour
- ○ Sugar-free squash

SNACKS

- ○ Sugar-free jelly
- ○ Plain popcorn
- ○ Olives in brine

FROZEN

- ○ Frozen vegetables

SEASONING & CONDIMENTS

- ○ Calorie controlled cooking spray
- ○ Stock cubes
- ○ Dried herbs and spices
- ○ Seasoning mixes
- ○ Sweet chilli sauce
- ○ Soy sauce
- ○ Olive oil
- ○ Salt and pepper

 Use the No Count list on page 110 as the inspiration for your shopping list.

Eating out

Don't put your social life on hold. Our top eating out tips will help you spot the smart choices on the menu.

1. Look up the menu online before you go and decide what to order before you set off. That way you won't be side-lined by what anyone else orders.

2. Ask for dressings, sauces and gravy to be served 'on the side' so you can decide how much of it you want to have.

3. Understand the lingo: smothered, rich, au gratin, glazed and creamy usually indicate high SmartPoints. Flame-grilled, poached, smoked, baked and grilled tend to be lower.

4. Don't be shy to ask for what you want – a salad instead of chips with your main course or vegetables served plain rather than swimming in butter. You pay the piper; you call the tune!

5. Resign from the clean plate club – you won't get told off for not finishing your food. Stop when you're comfortably full, not when you're stuffed.

6. Be salad savvy – creamy dressings and toppings like croutons, bacon, avocado, nuts and seeds tend to be high in SmartPoints. Simple, leafy salads topped with grilled chicken or fish are likely to be lower.

7. Use your weekly SmartPoints allowance – it's there to give you extra flexibility. So if it makes sense, put them in the bank and spend them at the restaurant.

8. Most important of all – enjoy yourself. If you've got enough SmartPoints in your budget and you want it – have it and love every bite of it. And if you do go over – get over it. Your next meal is the one that matters.

 Need quick answers? Find them 24/7 with Expert Chat on the Weight Watchers app or online at weightwatchers.com/uk

EATING OUT ON NO COUNT

It helps if you can pick the restaurant – as some are more 'No Count friendly' than others. We've put a list of the sorts of things you should look out for below. But don't be shy about asking how the food is cooked or requesting that your food is served the way you want it – grilled rather than fried, without butter or sauces, salads undressed, etc.

SCAN THE MENU FOR GOOD NO COUNT OPTIONS LIKE THESE:

- Jacket potatoes or boiled new potatoes without butter
- Grilled meat, fish, chicken or seafood
- Salads or grilled vegetables without butter or sauce
- Brown rice
- Wholewheat pasta
- Tea or coffee made with skimmed milk
- Fresh fruit platters

Get the inside track on eating out with our genius Eat Out guide*.

* Available to buy in your meeting or our online shop.

SECRET *weapons*

We're not going to suggest you run out and buy a huge number of gadgets but these are some of the **secret weapons that many people have come to rely on**. You probably have most of these knocking around in your kitchen already – so dig them out and put them to work.

A NON-STICK FRYING PAN. This makes it so much easier to drastically cut down (or even eliminate) added oils and fat when you're cooking. All you'll need to do is mist the pan with an oil spray or with calorie controlled cooking spray and you can fry eggs, brown meat and veg – do everything you usually do, but with far fewer SmartPoints.

AN OIL SPRAYER. It gives you all the taste of your favourite oil without all the SmartPoints. On average, 5 full sprays = 1 SmartPoints value. Spritz directly onto pans, trays and grills or onto salads & pasta. And you can flavour it up by sticking a sprig of rosemary or a clove of garlic into the jar.

KITCHEN SCALES + MEASURING SPOONS & CUPS. You don't have to become obsessive about it, but it does make sense to weigh & measure foods until you have a good handle on portion sizes, and then to do a re-check every now and then to make sure your portion sizes aren't creeping up.

STORAGE CONTAINERS. We're big fans of the 'cook once, eat twice' school for spending less time in the kitchen. That jumble of plastic boxes lurking at the back of your cupboard can come into their own now.

JULIENNE PEELER. Have you tried courgetti yet? If not, check out the recipe on page 76. It's like having your pasta and eating it, without spending any SmartPoints. And all you need is a julienne peeler (and a couple of courgettes). Or you could invest in a spiralizer.

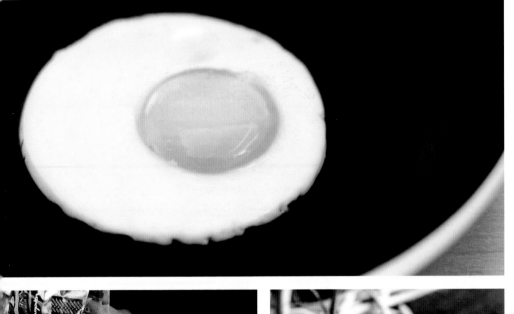

MINDFUL
eating

In our grab-and-go lives, food is often treated as mere fuel –
eaten in a rush without much thought. Multi-tasking while eating – whether
that's watching TV, checking in on Facebook, working on your laptop, reading
or writing a to-do list – can result in you eating more than you actually need.
When you take the time to focus on what's in front of you, something amazing
happens – **you begin to be satisfied with less**.

Give it a try – just start by committing to 'eating mindfully' for one meal
this week. You might just find that the short escape from busyness and mind
chatter makes for happier and healthier eating.

HERE ARE SOME TOP TIPS:

- Slow it down. Take an extra 10 minutes over your lunch.
- Focus on what's on your plate, not what's on a screen. That means no TV, no computer, no phone or tablet and no work.
- Eat at the table if you can (and definitely not standing up).
- Chew your food thoroughly. Don't pile your fork or spoon too high. Put your cutlery down between mouthfuls. Take breaths between mouthfuls.
- Tune into the textures, aromas and flavours. Take pleasure in discovering or rediscovering new and different foods.
- Wait 20 minutes after eating before you think about having a second portion. It takes a while for your stomach to send the 'I'm full' signal to your brain.
- Make the whole process of eating a ritual rather than a routine.

Food won't change your mood. Discover more in Smile.

NOW FOR THE
food

"PEOPLE WHO LOVE TO EAT
ARE ALWAYS THE BEST PEOPLE."
JULIA CHILD

Eating healthy delicious food shouldn't be hard work. **We think good food should be easy to prepare**.

On the following pages you'll find dozens of real-food meal ideas, tasty snacks and sweet treats. And if you hate to cook, don't worry – we've got a bunch of 'throw this and that together' meals that are ready in no time.

Our focus is on simple, everyday eating with the minimum of fuss. But we've snuck in a few indulgent (and seriously yummy) ideas too.

SIGN LANGUAGE

The number inside the SmartPoints coin tells you how many SmartPoints are in the food, meal or recipe.

A food, meal or recipe that's suitable for No Count. Find out more on page 11.

GF A meal that is gluten-free* or can be made gluten-free with a few simple swaps. So if we say soy sauce, make sure you use a gluten-free version.

V Vegetarian.

> BARGAIN HUNT: MOST FRUITS AND MOST VEGETABLES ARE ZERO SMARTPOINTS – THEY ARE ALWAYS A GOOD CHOICE. ENOUGH SAID.

 Look up the SmartPoints of your favourite food products with the Barcode Scanner on our Weight Watchers app (for Subscribers).

* If you're gluten-free: the gluten content of some convenience foods varies from brand to brand. If you are eating a gluten-free diet, make sure to read the labels of all food products to be sure they're gluten-free, especially for items like stock cubes, salad dressing, soy and Asian-style sauces, salsa and tomato sauce, yogurt and sour cream.

LET'S *eat*

Breakfast

It sets you up for the day. Anything goes but the more filling and nourishing, the better.

We've got loads of tasty and satisfying ideas for you here – from the 'grab & run' to the 'lazy weekend brunch' – **breakfast really can be the highlight of the day.**

toast

You pull it out of the toaster and load up with your favourite topping. Voila! Breakfast. **Here are some of our favourite things to put on toast.**

TAKE 1 MEDIUM SLICE OF GRANARY TOAST ③ AND TOP WITH:

Ⓥ A GOOD EGG: 1 medium egg cooked your favourite way - poached, fried or scrambled (without added oil – use calorie controlled cooking spray). Serve with grilled tomatoes and mushrooms on the side. (Add 2 SmartPoints values).

Ⓥ COTTAGE CHEESE: 2 tbsp reduced fat cottage cheese, sliced tomatoes and chopped cucumber (1 SmartPoints value).

Ⓥ HOT BANANA & BLUEBERRIES: Slice a ripe banana and layer onto your toast. Sprinkle with ¼ tsp sweetener and a pinch of cinnamon. Top with blueberries and pop under a hot grill for a couple of mins. (0 SmartPoints values).

SARDINES: Mash ½ can sardines in oil (drained) onto the toast, squeeze with lemon and then pop under a hot grill for 2 mins. (Add 2 SmartPoints values).

Ⓥ BEANS: Heat 3 tbsp baked beans, add a dash of Worcestershire sauce and spoon over your toast. (Add 3 SmartPoints values).

Ⓥ JAM, HONEY, PEANUT BUTTER OR MARMITE: Top your toast with 2 tsp reduced calorie jam or 1 tsp honey (Add 1 SmartPoints value) or 1 tsp smooth peanut butter (Add 2 SmartPoints values) or 1 tsp Marmite (0 SmartPoints values).

NO TOAST WITHOUT BUTTER?

That's fine with us! 1 tsp of butter adds 2 SmartPoints values. If you switch to low fat spread you can have 1 tsp for 1 SmartPoints value.

Ⓞ Choose calorie controlled brown bread and check the No Count list (page 110) for toppings (or use some of your weekly SmartPoints allowance).

WHAT A *smoothie*

Put your Nutribullet™ or blender to work and start the day with a healthy dose of veggies & fruit. These two smoothies are from our **Losing Weight the Smart Way** cookbook.

SPICED CELERY
Place a pear (de-seeded), 2 celery sticks, 2 handfuls of chopped kale and a small bunch of fresh parsley in a juicer and blend. Add a pinch of turmeric and a couple of tbsp of cold water to the machine and rinse through to thin the juice. **(Serves 1)**

RHUBARB & PEAR WITH HONEY *per serving*
Place 300g rhubarb in a small pan with 2 tbsp water, bring to the boil, cover and simmer for around 5 minutes until completely broken down. Cool slightly then push through a fine sieve to extract the juice, then cool completely. Juice 2 pears (de-seeded) with a small piece of peeled fresh root ginger and stir in 2 tsp honey. Add as much of the strained rhubarb juice as you like (it's quite tart so taste as you go). **(Serves 2)**

CEREAL *thrillers*

Nothing says 'quick & easy breakfast' like a **bowl of cereal**. And it's pretty easy to ring the changes and make that bowl **tasty and filling**.

POUR YOUR CHOSEN CEREAL INTO A BOWL:

30g bran flakes

30g corn flakes

20g puffed wheat

2 Shredded Wheat

TOP WITH:

¼ pint skimmed milk

¼ pint unsweetened soya milk

¼ pint semi skimmed milk

3 tbsp 0% fat natural Greek yogurt

THROW SOME FRUIT AT IT:

mixed berries

sliced banana

sliced apple

sliced pear

THEN MAKE IT EXTRA SPECIAL:

1 tbsp chopped almonds

pinch of cinnamon

pinch of nutmeg

1 tsp sweetener

OVERNIGHT *oats*

Meet the easiest breakfast ever. You mix a few ingredients together before you go to bed. In the morning you grab a spoon and tuck in. Great for taking to work too. **Oh - did we mention how gorgeous they are?**

FRENCH BERRY

Layer the oats, fromage frais and most of the berries in a jar or bowl. Cover and put in the fridge overnight. In the morning, stir to combine the layers, top with the remaining berries and tuck in.

Serves 1

35g oats
200g fat free natural
  fromage frais
200g berries
  (any you choose)

BANANA HONEY

Combine the first 4 ingredients in a small jar and put the lid on tightly. Give it a good shake and then put in the fridge overnight. In the morning, top with banana and tuck in.

Serves 1

35g oats
100ml skimmed milk
½ tsp vanilla extract
1 tsp honey
1 banana, sliced

GREEK BERRY

Combine all the ingredients except a few of the raspberries in a small jar. Cover and put in the fridge overnight. In the morning, top with the remaining berries and tuck in.

Serves 1

35g oats
60ml skimmed milk
60g 0% fat natural
  Greek yogurt
1 tsp maple syrup or honey
100g raspberries

 Get loads more breakfast recipe inspiration
online at weightwatchers.com/uk

BREAKFAST BERRY
pancakes

  per serving

Serves 4

Put the flour, sugar and salt in a mixing bowl and make a well in the middle. Put the milk, egg yolk and vanilla extract into a jug and stir. Whisk the milk mixture into the flour mixture until you have a smooth batter. In a separate bowl, whisk the egg white to soft peaks and then gently fold into the batter with half the blueberries.

Heat a large, non-stick frying pan and mist with cooking spray. Put 2 spoonfuls of the pancake mixture into the pan. Once you see bubbles forming (1-2 mins), flip the pancakes and cook on the other sides. Keep the cooked pancakes warm while you make 3 further batches (total 8 pancakes).

Combine the rest of the blueberries with the sliced bananas. Serve 2 pancakes per person topped with fruit, fromage frais and a drizzle of honey.

125g self-raising flour
a pinch of salt
2 tsp caster sugar
1 egg, separated
150ml skimmed milk
1 tsp vanilla extract
calorie-controlled cooking spray
250g blueberries
2 bananas, sliced
120g fat free natural fromage frais
4 tsp honey to drizzle

PERFECT FOR A LAZY WEEKEND MORNING. KIDS LOVE THEM AND IT BRINGS OUT THE KID IN GROWN UPS TOO!

Porridge

   *per serving*

Serves 1

Place the water in the pan with the oats and bring to the boil. Turn the heat down to a simmer and cook for 5 mins, stirring often. Serve in a bowl with your choice of topping.

35g porridge oats
250ml water

FOR 0 SMARTPOINTS VALUES ADD:

- Your choice of fresh or frozen fruit
- ½ tsp ground cinnamon
- ½ tsp orange zest

FOR 1 SMARTPOINTS VALUE ADD:

- 1 tbsp fat free natural yogurt
- 1 tsp honey
- 1 tsp toasted flaked almonds

SMOKED *haddock* FLORENTINE

   per serving

Serves 2

Put the haddock fillets in a frying pan and just cover with boiling water. Simmer gently for 5 mins until fish is opaque. Meanwhile, poach the eggs for 3-4 mins (add a few drops of vinegar to the water). Whilst the eggs are poaching, wilt the spinach (in a pan or microwave) and squeeze out excess water. Divide the spinach between 2 warm plates, top with the haddock and poached eggs. Season and serve.

2 x 175g skinless smoked haddock fillets
a few drops of vinegar
2 medium eggs
300g young leaf spinach

SMART COOKED

breakfast

 per serving

Serves 2

Preheat the grill. Put the sausages on the grill rack and grill for 5 mins.

Put the mushrooms and stock into a pan, bring to the boil, reduce heat and simmer for 5-6 mins, stirring occasionally.

After the sausages have been on for 5 mins, turn and add the bacon medallions and tomatoes, cook for 5 mins until crispy, turning the bacon once.

Meanwhile, spray a non-stick frying pan with the cooking spray, heat for a few seconds then crack in the eggs and cook over a medium heat for 2-3 mins to set them, then finish off under the grill while you warm the baked beans.

Share everything between 2 warm plates, season and serve.

150g mushrooms, sliced
100ml fresh vegetable stock
2 medium reduced fat pork sausages
4 bacon medallion rashers
10 cherry tomatoes, on the vine
calorie controlled cooking spray
2 medium eggs
220g can reduced sugar & salt baked beans

light meals

Whatever you choose, pack it with veggies or have a big salad on the side – it's the healthy way to stay satisfied.

We've got a brilliant collection of 'want to eat them right now' light meals for you here. And if you often eat al-desko you'll adore our 'salad jars'.

READY IN 10
TORTILLA *pizzas*

V MARGHERITA (6) SmartPoints *per serving*

Preheat the oven to 200°C, Gas Mark 6. Put the tortillas on a large baking sheet and spread them with the passata. Scatter the mozzarella over and season. Cook for 5 mins or until hot through. Serve with the rocket scattered over.

Serves 2

2 soft flour tortillas
6 tbsp tomato passata
80g light mozzarella
  cheese, diced
handful rocket leaves

V (6) SmartPoints VEGGIE-DELIGHT As above + diced red pepper, sliced spring onion, diced courgette and sliced mushrooms.

(6) SmartPoints GO HAWAIIAN As above + 2 rings canned pineapple in juice, drained and cubed plus 30g wafer thin ham.

(5) SmartPoints PRAWN, COURGETTE & PESTO Leave out the passata, mozzarella & rocket. Instead spread tortillas with 1 tbsp fresh pesto. Top with 1 small courgette, coarsely grated and 120g cooked peeled prawns. Serve with chopped parsley scattered over.

PICK & MIX *salad*

Kick it off with a bunch of delicious **zero SmartPoints** soft, herby or crunchy leaves, colourful peppers, crisp apple slices, juicy tomato halves, sweet carrot batons, cool cucumber slices, blanched green beans or sugar snaps, tangy onion slivers – there are no rules, anything goes.

THEN TAKE IT UP A *level*

Make it more filling and more delicious by adding one or two of these delicious things to the bowl...

1 boiled egg — 2 SmartPoints value

roasted veg (no added oil) — 0 SmartPoints value

1 tbsp chickpeas — 1 SmartPoints value

40g feta cheese — 4 SmartPoints value

10 olives in brine, drained — 1 SmartPoints value

70g tuna (in spring water, drained) — 1 SmartPoints value

medium chicken breast (no skin) — 2 SmartPoints value

46g wafer thin ham — 1 SmartPoints value

fresh pineapple — 0 SmartPoints value

4 anchovies — 0 SmartPoints value

100g peeled prawns — 1 SmartPoints value

½ avocado — 5 SmartPoints value

AND NOW DRESS *it up*

Bring it all together with a lovely dressing. Mix all the ingredients together, stir until blended and pour over the salad. All serve 1.

V CHEAT'S VINAIGRETTE
2 tbsp rice wine vinegar, 2 tsp Dijon mustard, pinch of garlic powder, freshly ground black pepper.

ORIENTAL
Big squeeze of lime juice, ½ tsp fish sauce, ½ tsp rice vinegar, pinch of sugar, 1 red chilli (de-seeded and finely chopped).

V YOGURT ①
25g fat-free natural yogurt, ½ tsp lemon juice, pinch smoked paprika, ¼ garlic clove (grated).

V CREAMY ①
1 tbsp fat free natural fromage frais, a of squeeze lemon juice, pinch of chilli powder, freshly ground black pepper.

HERE'S ONE WE MADE *earlier*

GF **O** CHICKEN & EGG SALAD ③
Toss together salad leaves, spring onions, cucumber and red pepper. Add 30g wafer thin chicken and 1 boiled egg (sliced). Top with Creamy Dressing (above). **Yum**.

Omelettes

Easy to make, good for you, **low in SmartPoints** and oh so versatile. Omelettes pack **a delicious protein punch** and are great at lunch, breakfast or supper.

BASIC 2 EGG OMELETTE

Serves 1

2 medium eggs
calorie controlled
cooking spray

Preheat the grill. Whisk the eggs with seasoning and set aside. Choose your fillings, prepare them and add to a non-stick frying pan (misted with cooking spray). Once cooked, pour in the eggs, swirl to cover the pan and cook on a medium heat. Tip the pan from side to side to allow the uncooked egg to run over the edges of the cooked egg. Cook until almost completely set, then take off the heat and finish under the grill.

GORGEOUS FILLINGS

The SmartPoints below are for the basic 2 egg omelette + the fillings:

HAM & TOMATO

1 red pepper, 2 spring onions, 60g wafer thin ham, 2 tsp fresh herbs, 4 cherry tomatoes.

PRAWN & CHIVE

100g peeled prawns and 1 tbsp chopped chives.

CHICKEN & MUSHROOM

½ medium chicken breast (diced) and a handful of chopped mushrooms.

FETA & VEG

30g crumbled feta cheese plus a mix of your favourite veg (chopped or shredded) – peppers, spring onions, mushrooms and spinach are nice here.

SALAD IN A *jar*

The Salad Jar solves all your **'on-the-go lunch'** problems. It's portable and healthy. You can make it the night before and have an extra 5 minutes in bed. **There's lots of room for variety so you'll never get bored**. And best of all – layer it up right and there'll be no more limp lettuce.

HOW TO:

Put the dressing ingredients in the jar and shake to combine. Layer the other salad ingredients in the bowl in the order listed in each recipe. Seal and put in the fridge for up to 24 hours. Take to work. Shake. And tuck in. (**All recipes serve 1**).

LEAVES &
TOPPINGS

VEGGIES &
PROTEINS

DRESSING &
WET INGREDIENTS

DRY

WET

SUNSHINE VEG

DRESSING
¼ tsp honey
juice of ½ lemon
1 tsp olive oil

SALAD
40g chickpeas
25g red cabbage, thinly
  sliced
3" chunk of cucumber,
  sliced
1 small carrot, grated
½ sliced red pepper
½ sliced yellow pepper
handful of rocket leaves
½ tbsp sunflower seeds

CHICK CHICKEN

DRESSING
2 tbsp fat free natural fromage frais
½ tsp Dijon or grainy mustard
½ tsp balsamic vinegar
freshly ground black pepper

SALAD
1 medium cooked skinless chicken
    breast, cubed
1 small carrot, grated
100g chickpeas in water, drained
3" chunk of cucumber, cubed
50g green beans, halved,
    pre-cooked al dente and cooled
25g rocket or other salad greens
1 tsp grated parmesan

 Leave out the parmesan

TUNA RAINBOW

DRESSING
1 tsp sesame oil
zest and juice of ½ an orange
dash of soy sauce

SALAD
130g tuna steak in
    spring water, drained
30g dry quinoa, cooked
    according to pack
    instructions and left to
    cool completely
70g cherry tomatoes, halved
1 small carrot, grated
1 small beetroot, grated
25g baby spinach or
    other salad greens

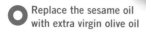 **Replace the sesame oil
with extra virgin olive oil**

Sandwiches
& WRAPS

TAKE 2 MEDIUM SLICES OF GRANARY BREAD (5) AND ADD THE FOLLOWING TO CREATE A MASTERPIECE:

(V) EGG 'MAYONNAISE': 1 medium hard boiled egg (cooled) mashed with 1 tbsp natural quark; season (a pinch of cayenne is good here), stir through some snipped chives. Pile onto the bread with cucumber and salad leaves. (Add 3 SmartPoints values)

HAM SALSA: 60g wafer thin ham, 2 tbsp fat free tomato salsa, some thin slices of red onion and cucumber. (Add 2 SmartPoints values)

CORONATION CHICKEN: Mix 2 tbsp fat free natural fromage frais with ½ tsp curry powder. Add 60g wafer thin chicken and stir to coat. Load up your sandwich with the chicken and add tomatoes, cucumber and lettuce. (Add 2 SmartPoints values)

TURKEY CLUB TOASTIE: Toast the bread. Mix together 2 tbsp natural quark, ½ tsp Dijon mustard, a squeeze of lemon juice. Season, stir and spread the mixture over a slice of toast. Pile on 50g cooked sliced skinless turkey breast and 2 grilled smoked bacon medallions followed by a sliced tomato and some lettuce. Top with another slice of toast. (Add 4 SmartPoints values)

CHANGE IT UP.

TRY PUMPERNICKEL: It's really filling and has a lovely, slightly sweet taste. 2 medium slices for 3 SmartPoints values.

WRAP IT UP: Have a Weight Watchers Wrap for 3 SmartPoints values.

HAVE A BAGEL: Choose a Weight Watchers Bagel for 5 SmartPoints values.

GO THIN: Have you tried Sandwich Thins yet? At 3 SmartPoints values, they are a good sandwich option.

INSTANT noodle jars

This is a great no-fuss lunch. Fill the jar (make sure it's heatproof) the night before and pop it in the fridge. In the morning, remember to take it with you. And when you're ready for lunch, add boiling water and make your colleagues green with envy.

Serves 1

Put the dressing ingredients at the bottom of a Kilner jar with a fitting hinged lid. Add the rice noodles and layer up the vegetables in the order given. Store in the fridge. When you're ready to eat, fill the jar with boiling water and screw on the lid. Leave for 8 mins or until noodles are tender. **SLURP!**

DRESSING
1 tsp ginger, grated
1 tsp miso paste
½ tsp sesame oil
1 tsp soy sauce
½ small chilli, de-seeded
& sliced

NOODLES & VEG
40g fine rice noodles
1 large handful spinach leaves,
½ small courgette, finely sliced
½ small carrot, grated
½ red pepper, finely sliced
3 spring onions, finely sliced

MAKE IT YOUR OWN:

MAX UP THE VEG: Anything goes – sugar-snap peas, courgettes, broccoli florets, baby corn, mushrooms, whatever takes your fancy.

DRESSING: Zing it up with lime juice or curry powder.

MORE PROTEIN: Add wafer thin chicken or ham (1 SmartPoints for 46g). Make sure you keep the jar in the fridge and eat it within 24 hours if using ham or chicken.

PERFECT *jackets*

Preheat the oven to 220°C, Gas Mark 7. Take one 200g baking potato (or sweet potato) and prick all over with a fork, place on a plate and microwave on high (850W) for 2 mins. Turn it over and microwave for a further 2 mins or until tender. Transfer to a baking sheet and spray with calorie controlled cooking spray. Season and bake in the oven for 20 mins to crisp the skin.

PUSHED FOR TIME? Microwave only for 8 mins, turning halfway.

TIME ON YOUR HANDS? Oven only for 1 hr 15 mins or until skin is crisp and flesh is soft.

All recipes **serve 1** and are based on a medium (200g) potato for 5 SmartPoints values. A medium sweet potato (150g) is 5 SmartPoints values.

JACKET POTATO BURGER

Season 125g extra lean beef mince then press into a patty. Place on a foil tray under a pre-heated grill for 10-15 mins, turning halfway, until cooked through. Spread 1 tbsp fresh tomato salsa (no added oil) over the burger and grill for another min. Cut the jacket in half, top with a sliced tomato, 1 tbsp fat free natural yogurt and the cooked burger. Serve with a salad or some steamed green beans.

TUNA. LIME & CORIANDER

½ tin tuna in spring water (drained) flaked through with the juice of ½ a lime, 1 thinly sliced red pepper, some cucumber chunks and a small handful of fresh coriander leaves. Stir together and pile onto your jacket. Serve with a big green salad.

FRUITY COLESLAW

Mix together a small handful of grated cabbage (white, red or a mixture), 1 small carrot (peeled and grated), ½ apple (peeled, cored and grated) 1 fresh pineapple slice (finely chopped), 2 spring onions (finely sliced) and 2 tbsp reduced fat mayonnaise. Pile onto your jacket.

PRAWN COCKTAIL

Mix 3 tbsp fat free natural fromage frais with ½ tsp tomato purée and season with a dash of Tabasco. Add 100g peeled prawns and 1 tbsp chopped chives. Pile onto your jacket and serve with a tomato and onion salad.

SPEEDY YUMMY *gnocchi*

  *per serving*

Warm a large, non-stick frying pan and mist with the cooking spray. Add the stir-fry vegetables and cook until al dente, about 8 mins. Meanwhile, cook the gnocchi according to pack instructions. Add to the veg along with the pesto and stir to coat.

Serve in bowls with the cheese strewn across the top and a green salad on the side.

Serves 2

250g fresh gnocchi
calorie controlled cooking spray
200g stir-fry vegetables (choose your favourite mix at the supermarket)
1 tbsp red pesto
1 tbsp hard Italian cheese (vegetarian)
green salad to serve

READY IN 10 MINS

FETA STUFFED *peppers*

  per serving

Serves 2

Preheat the oven to 200°C, Gas Mark 6.

Mist a baking tray with calorie controlled spray. Place 4 red pepper halves on the tray. Stuff each half with 4 tomatoes, a quarter of the garlic and a quarter of the feta cheese (crumbled), a couple of basil leaves, a pinch of chilli flakes and a good grinding of black pepper.

Mist again with the cooking spray. Bake for 45 mins.

Divide between 2 plates, garnish with basil leaves and serve with a green salad.

*2 red peppers, halved
and de-seeded
16 cherry tomatoes
2 garlic cloves, peeled
and crushed
100g feta cheese
1 tsp chilli flakes
(optional)
fresh basil leaves
calorie controlled cooking
spray
green salad to serve*

THREE
super soups

 *per serving*

ROASTED BUTTERNUT SQUASH SOUP

Preheat the oven to 190°C, Gas Mark 5. Put all the vegetables on a large non-stick baking tray and spray with cooking spray. Roast for 45 mins until golden and tender, stirring halfway through.

Transfer to a blender and whizz in batches with a little of the boiling water until smooth. Transfer to a large pan and add the remaining water. Gently heat the soup until just before boiling, then season and serve.

Serves 6

1 red onion, chopped
1 garlic clove, halved
1 fresh rosemary sprig,
   leaves only
800g butternut squash,
   peeled, de-seeded and
   cut into small chunks
2 carrots, peeled and
   chopped roughly
½ swede, peeled and
   chopped roughly
calorie controlled
   cooking spray
1 litre boiling water

Get loads more recipe inspiration
online at weightwatchers.com/uk

 *per serving*

THAI VEGETABLE BROTH

Serves 1

Place the mushrooms, chilli, lemon grass and ginger in a lidded saucepan with 2 tbsp of the stock. Cover and cook for 4 mins. Add the rest of the stock, the soy sauce and baby corn. Cover again and cook for 3 mins. Add the mangetout and cook for a final 2 mins.

Stir in the lime juice, ladle into a bowl and serve scattered with the coriander.

75g mushrooms, sliced
½ red chilli de-seeded and sliced
½ stick of fresh lemon grass, chopped finely
1cm fresh root ginger, peeled and cut into matchsticks
400ml vegetable stock
1 tbsp soy sauce
50g baby corn sliced
40g mangetout, halved
juice of ½ lime
2 tbsp chopped fresh coriander

 per serving

MARVELLOUS MINESTRONE

Serves 6

Put the first 10 ingredients into a large lidded saucepan. Bring to the boil, stirring occasionally. Partially cover, then reduce the heat and simmer for 20-25 mins, until the vegetables are tender.

Add the pasta shapes and green beans. Stir well, then cook for a further 8-10 mins, until the pasta is tender. Season then serve, topped with a few basil leaves.

This minestrone is marvellous because it fills you up and keeps you satisfied. It's a great take-to-work option too.

1 large onion, chopped
2 garlic cloves, crushed
2 large carrots, chopped
3 celery sticks, sliced thinly
½ swede, chopped
1½ litres vegetable stock
410g can borlotti beans, drained
400g can chopped tomatoes
2 tbsp tomato purée
1 tbsp dried mixed Italian herbs
50g dried small pasta shapes
100g fine green beans, trimmed and sliced
fresh basil leaves to garnish

TANDOORI *chicken*

WITH SPICED YOGURT

   per serving

Serves 2

Mix the spices, garlic, ginger and lemon juice with ½ the yogurt in a small bowl (reserve the rest for the sauce). Make 3 diagonal slits into each chicken breast (be careful not to go all the way through). Coat the chicken with the spiced yogurt, cover and leave to marinade (at least 30 mins but up to 24 hours).

Preheat the oven to 220°C, Gas Mark 7.

Make the Yogurt Sauce by mixing together all the ingredients in a small bowl, then put in the fridge to chill.

Once the oven is hot, remove the chicken from its marinade and place on a roasting rack inside a pan. Bake for 12 mins on each side, or until cooked through, turning once. Serve with the Yogurt Sauce and a big salad.

150g pot 0% fat natural
  Greek yogurt
½ tsp ground cumin
½ tsp paprika
1 tsp garam masala
1 tsp curry powder
½ tsp cayenne pepper
2 tsp grated ginger root
2 garlic cloves, grated
2 medium skinless,
  boneless chicken
  breasts
juice of ½ lemon

YOGURT SAUCE
bunch of fresh mint,
  finely chopped
½ cucumber, sliced into
  half-moons

Serving suggestion: Add 75g cooked brown rice per person for 3 SmartPoints or Cauliflower Rice for 0 SmartPoints – see recipe on page 73.

Looking for some new chicken recipes?
Find inspiration online at weightwatchers.com/uk

SIMPLY LOVELY RICE PAPER
prawn rolls

  per serving

Serves 4

Combine the ingredients for the dipping sauce with 2 tbsp water and set to one side. Place the rice noodles in a bowl and cover with boiling water. Stir and soak for about 5 minutes, or until tender. Refresh under cold water and drain well before placing in a bowl.

Add the beansprouts, carrot, spring onions, prawns, basil, fish sauce and lime zest. Combine well and set aside.

Fill a bowl wide enough to fit a whole rice paper with cold water and add one of the rice papers. Carefully dunk under the water for a couple of minutes until completely softened. Shake dry, then place on a piece of kitchen paper on the work surface.

Spoon an eighth of the filling in a mound along the centre of the rice paper circle, leaving a 4 cm gap at each end. Fold the sides over the filling and then roll up into a tube shape similar to a spring roll. Set to one side and repeat with the remaining rice papers. Serve with the dipping sauce.

From our gorgeous cookbook – Losing Weight the Smart Way*

50g Thai rice noodles
50g beansprouts
*1 carrot, halved and cut
 into very fine matchsticks*
*4 spring onions, halved
 and sliced*
*200g peeled and cooked
 prawns, defrosted if frozen*
3 tbsp chopped fresh basil
1 tsp Thai fish sauce
zest of 1 lime
8 x 22 cm rice papers

FOR THE DIPPING SAUCE
juice of 2 limes
2 tbsp Thai fish sauce
*½ red chilli, de-seeded and
 chopped very finely*
1 tbsp brown sugar
2 tbsp torn fresh coriander
*1 tbsp mirin or medium
 sherry*
1 garlic clove, crushed

* Available to buy in your meeting or our online shop.

Main meals

Make meals with substance and then make the most of them by taking the time to truly savour what you are eating.

We've got a whole range of delicious, hearty and flavour-packed main meals for you here. And your family will love them too. Result.

ARE YOU EATING MINDFULLY?
FIND OUT ON PAGE 24

pick & mix
SUPPERS

Take 1 **protein hero**; add 1 **smart side** and bring it to life with 1 **lovely sauce**. That's a load of yummy supper combinations right here. They're all easy to make, family-friendly, low in SmartPoints and super delicious. **Enjoy!**

PROTEIN HEROES

SMART SIDES

SMART SAUCES

ALL EASY TO MAKE AND DELICIOUS - TURN PAGE FOR RECIPES.

5 PROTEIN *heroes*

LEMON CHICKEN

Lay 1 medium (165g) skinless, boneless chicken breast between 2 slices of cling-film and tenderise (bash with a rolling pin) until flat and even. Put 1 tbsp milk in a shallow dish, add the chicken and turn to coat. Put the zest of ½ a lemon, 1 tsp plain flour and ½ tsp chopped thyme leaves on a plate, stir to mix. Lift the chicken from the milk and add it to the flour mixture, turn to coat and shake off any excess. Heat ½ tsp olive oil in a non-stick frying pan. Add the chicken and fry, turning regularly, for 5-6 mins until cooked through and golden. **(Serves 1)**

QUORN MEATFREE CHICKEN FILLET

Cook according to pack instructions. **(Serves 1)**

SAUSAGES

Pre-heat grill to medium. Place 2 reduced fat pork sausages on a sheet of foil under the grill for 12-15 mins or until cooked, turning twice. **(Serves 1)**

SEARED TUNA

Season a 140g tuna steak and mist with calorie controlled cooking spray. Cook the tuna on a hot griddle pan over a high heat for 2 mins each side for medium or until cooked to your liking. (You can boost the flavour by marinating the tuna in a mixture of 1 tsp tamari soy sauce, 1 tbsp lemon juice, ¼ tsp ground ginger for 15 mins). **(Serves 1)**

AROMATIC PORK

Rub 1 tsp harissa paste onto a medium (130g) pork escalope. Warm a non-stick frying pan and mist with calorie controlled cooking spray. Cook the pork over a medium heat for 5-6 mins, turning once. Remove and leave to rest for 2 mins. **(Serves 1)**

5 SMART *sides*

Ⓥ LEEK & POTATO GRATIN ③ *per serving*

Preheat the oven to 190°C, Gas Mark 5. Put 450g thinly sliced potatoes in a saucepan with 600ml vegetable stock. Bring to the boil, then simmer for 8 mins or until just tender. Drain and reserve a little of the stock. Meanwhile, heat 1 tsp olive oil in a non-stick frying plan, add 3 thinly sliced leeks and gently cook for 8 mins or until softened. Arrange the potatoes in a 1.5 litre gratin dish and scatter the leeks on top. Combine 2 tbsp crème fraîche with 2 tbsp chopped fresh parsley and 2 tbsp of the reserved stock, season and pour over the vegetables. Bake for 25 mins until just golden. **(Serves 6)**

ⒼⒻ Ⓥ Ⓞ SPICED ROAST VEGETABLES ⓪ *per serving*

Preheat the oven to 200°C, Gas Mark 6. Tip 300g butternut squash (peeled and chopped) and 300g carrots (peeled and chopped) into a large roasting tin and spray with calorie controlled cooking spray. Roast in the oven for 15 mins. Add 1 courgette (sliced), 1 yellow and 1 red pepper (sliced) to the tin; sprinkle with 1 tsp chilli flakes, 1 tsp cumin seeds and a few sprigs of fresh thyme. Stir to mix and then return to the oven for another 20 mins or until the vegetables are tender. Add 12 cherry tomatoes to the tin, season and roast for 5 more mins. **(Serves 4)**

GF V O ROOT VEGETABLE MASH (3) *per serving*

Put 500g ready prepared carrot and swede and 500g potatoes (peeled & chopped) into a saucepan. Cover with boiling water and bring to the boil. Cover and simmer for about 15 mins, until the vegetables are tender. Drain in a colander, return to the saucepan, season and mash thoroughly. **(Serves 4)**

GF V O FENNEL ROASTED PEPPERS (1) *per serving*

Preheat the oven to 200°C, Gas Mark 6. Place 4 red pepper halves (de-seeded), 2 fennel bulbs (cut into thin wedges), 16 cherry tomatoes, 2 red onions (cut into thin wedges) and 4 garlic cloves on a roasting tray and mist with calorie controlled cooking spray. Scatter with fresh thyme, season and roast for 30 mins until cooked and slightly charred. Remove the garlic cloves, squeeze out the flesh and combine with 2 tbsp balsamic vinegar. Fill the pepper halves with the vegetables and drizzle with the balsamic dressing. **(Serves 4)**

GF V O CAULIFLOWER RICE (0) *per serving*

Blitz 1 cauliflower (cut into florets) in food processor for 30 seconds or until it resembles fine rice or couscous. (Alternatively grate the cauliflower using the coarse side of a box grater). Put the cauliflower 'rice' in a heatproof bowl, cover with cling film, pierce and then microwave for 3 mins on high, mixing the 'rice' halfway through cooking. Add flavour by stirring one or more of the following through after cooking: chopped herbs, 1 tsp of cumin, curry powder, paprika or coriander. **(Serves 4)**

5 SMART *sauces*

V O ZINGY TOMATO SAUCE *per serving*

Mist a non-stick frying pan with calorie controlled spray and warm over a medium heat. Fry 1 onion (finely chopped) for 5 mins till softened then add a 400g can chopped tomatoes, 1 tsp chilli flakes, 1 tsp balsamic vinegar, 1 tsp soy sauce and a few sprigs of thyme. Bring to the boil and simmer for 15 mins. Season and serve. **(Serves 4)**

V HONEY & MUSTARD SAUCE *per serving*

Melt 3 tbsp low-fat olive oil spread in a small pan. Add 1½ tbsp white wine vinegar, 1 tbsp Dijon mustard and 2 tsp clear honey. In a small bowl combine ½ tsp cornflour with 1½ tbsp water and then add to the pan. Bring to the boil, then simmer for 1-2 mins until slightly thickened. Season and serve. **(Serves 4)**

V O MUSHROOM SAUCE *per serving*

Heat a non-stick frying pan and add mist with calorie controlled cooking spray. Add 200g sliced mushrooms; 1 garlic clove (crushed) and 2 spring onions (finely sliced). Cook until lightly browned. Add 100ml vegetable stock, bring to the boil and simmer for 3 mins. Remove from the heat and stir in 100g 0% fat natural Greek yogurt and 2 tbsp chopped parsley. **(Serves 4)**

V CREAMY WHITE WINE SAUCE *per serving*

Heat a small pan over a low heat and mist with calorie controlled cooking spray. Add 1 finely chopped shallot and soften for 5 mins. Add 75ml white wine, bring to the boil and simmer for 5 mins or until reduced by two-thirds. Add 150ml vegetable stock and 3 tbsp single cream and stir. Simmer gently for 7 mins or until thickened. Season, stir through some chopped chives and serve. **(Serves 4)**

GOOD OLD 'BISTO' GRAVY *per serving*

50ml portion of Bisto Favourite Gravy Granules made according to pack instructions. **(Serves 1)**

pasta
OR
courgetti
3 WAYS

Pasta makes a lovely supper - simple, satisfying and versatile. But **have you tried courgetti** yet? Simple, satisfying, versatile **AND zero SmartPoints**. It's a delicious alternative so mix it up.

V O WHOLEWHEAT PASTA 5 SmartPoints value

60g (dry weight) per person. Bring a large pan of water to the boil, add the pasta and cook according to packet instructions.

GF V O COURGETTI 0 SmartPoints value

Allow 1 medium-large courgette per person. Use a julienne peeler to turn the courgette into thin spaghetti-like strips – this is courgetti. Or you can use a vegetable peeler to slice the courgettes lengthways into very wide ribbons, which you can then slice in half (a bit like tagliatelle). Put the courgetti in a large bowl, pour boiling water over, leave to stand for 4 mins to soften and heat through.

QUICK BEEF BOLOGNESE *per serving*

Heat a saucepan, add 500g extra lean minced beef and sear over a high heat without moving for 40 seconds. Stir and then cook for 4 mins until browned. Add 1 grated onion, 1 diced red pepper, a 400g can of chopped tomatoes and 2 tbsp tomato purée. Bring to the boil. Add 1 tbsp dried mixed Italian herbs and 200g sliced mushrooms and stir. Reduce the heat and simmer for 15 mins. Season to taste and serve. **(Serves 4)**

QUICK PRAWN & TOMATO *per serving*

Heat a saucepan and mist with calorie controlled cooking spray. Add 300g ripe tomatoes (chopped roughly), ½ a red chilli (de-seeded and sliced) and cook over a medium heat for 4 mins. Add 225g raw peeled prawns and a 4 tbsp water. Cover the pan and cook for 3 mins, stirring once or twice, until the prawns are cooked and pink. Season and serve garnished with grated lemon zest. **(Serves 2)**

QUICK PUTTANESCA *per serving*

Heat 1 tbsp olive oil in a non-stick frying pan over a medium heat. Fry 1 thinly sliced onion for 5 mins until soft. Add a grated garlic clove and cook for another min. Add 2 tbsp capers, 400g can chopped tomatoes, 4 whole roasted peppers (from a jar, packed in brine, drained and chopped) and 16 black olives (from a jar, in brine, pitted and halved) and cook for a few mins more until heated through. Season, sprinkle with chopped parsley and serve with pasta or courgetti. **(Serves 4)**

For all: Enjoy with a lovely big salad.

steak 'N' SIDES

  *per serving*

Serves 2

Boil the potatoes until tender, about 15 mins. Meanwhile, put the mushrooms in a saucepan with 200ml boiling water, crumble in the stock cube, heat & simmer gently for 10 mins.

When the potatoes have been cooking for 5 mins, preheat a non-stick frying pan. Mist the steaks with cooking spray, add to the pan and cook for 3-4 mins each side or until done to your liking. Remove from the pan, cover with foil and leave to rest.

Cook the tomatoes in the frying pan for 1-2 mins. Drain the potatoes and mushrooms and serve up.

*300g new potatoes
 (halved)
350g mushrooms, sliced
1 stock cube
2 x 150g lean fillet steaks
calorie controlled cooking
 spray
2 bunches cherry
 tomatoes on the vine
steamed green beans
Dijon mustard (optional)*

BEEF *stew*

 per serving

Preheat the oven to 150°C, Gas Mark 2. Mist a casserole with cooking spray and brown the onion, celery and carrots over a high heat for 4 mins. Add the garlic and cook for 1 min.

Meanwhile, combine the flour and cinnamon. Toss the beef in the spiced flour to coat, then add to the casserole along with the purée and vinegar. Pour in the wine and stock and sprinkle with thyme. Bring to the boil, cover and cook in the oven for 1½ hours until tender. Serve with green veg.

Serves 4

calorie controlled cooking spray
1 onion, chopped
2 celery sticks, chopped
4 carrots, chopped
2 garlic cloves, crushed
1 tbsp plain flour
1 tsp ground cinnamon
500g cubed lean beef stewing steak
2 tbsp tomato purée
3 tbsp balsamic vinegar
125ml red wine
400ml beef stock
¼ tsp dried thyme
fresh thyme leaves steamed green veg

ROAST *chicken*
AND ALL THE TRIMMINGS

 per serving

Serves 4

Preheat the oven to 180°C, Gas Mark 4. Slice one half of the lemon into 4 thin round slices. Loosen the skin of the chicken and place the lemon slices and the bay leaves under the skin. Put the remaining lemon half and the garlic in the chicken cavity. Spray with cooking spray and season.

Place in a roasting tin and roast on the middle shelf for 1 hour 15 mins, occasionally basting with the juices.

When the chicken has been cooking for 20 mins, put the potatoes in a pan with cold water, bring to the boil and simmer for 10 mins. Drain and shake to rough up the edges. Meanwhile, heat the oil in a roasting tin in the top shelf of the oven (above the chicken) until very hot. Add the potatoes to the oil, shake to coat and add the garlic clove.

The chicken is ready when the juices run clear (insert a skewer into the thickest part of the thigh).

Turn the oven up to 220°C, Gas Mark 7, remove the chicken from the oven, transfer to a warm plate and cover with foil. At this point, turn the potatoes.

After the chicken has rested for 15 mins, the potatoes should be crisp and golden. Carve, removing the skin and serve 80g per person with potatoes, vegetables and gravy.

1 large lemon, cut in half
1.5kg chicken
4 bay leaves
1 head of garlic, cut in half crossways
calorie controlled cooking spray

POTATOES
450g King Edward potatoes, peeled
1 bay leaf
1 tbsp olive oil
1 garlic clove

TO SERVE
steamed vegetables
50ml of Bisto Favourite gravy per person

 Find loads more family-friendly recipe inspiration online at weightwatchers.com/uk

Veggie FILO TART

  *per serving*

Serves 4

Preheat the oven to 220°C, Gas Mark 7. Mist a large baking sheet with cooking spray. Lay 2 sheets of filo on the sheet and spray with cooking spray. Lay the other 2 sheets on top and spray again. Scrunch up the edges to form a border and bake for 3-4 mins.

Boil the asparagus for 2 mins and drain. Beat the egg, crème fraîche and herbs together and season. Take the filo tart out of the oven and pour the egg mixture on top. Scatter the vegetables over and bake for a further 10-12 mins until the egg is set. Cool for a few mins, cut into quarters and serve warm or cold with a green salad.

calorie controlled cooking
  spray
4 x 45g Jus Rol filo
  pastry, thawed if frozen
150g fine asparagus
  (or green beans
  or mangetout)
1 large courgette, sliced
4 spring onions, sliced
8 cherry tomatoes,
  halved
1 large egg
100g reduced fat crème
  fraîche
1 tsp dried oregano
green salad to serve

COTTAGE *pie*

 *per serving*

Cook the sweet potatoes, carrots and cauliflower in boiling water until tender – about 20 mins. Meanwhile, heat a large saucepan and add the mince beef in batches, cooking over a high heat until browned. Add all the veg and the herbs to the beef with 400ml water and bring to the boil. Simmer, partially covered, for 20 mins.

Preheat the grill and warm a large baking dish under it for 2 mins. Drain and mash the sweet potatoes and season. Sprinkle the gravy granules onto the beef mixture and stir till thickened. Tip the beef into the dish, spread the mash on top and grill till lightly browned. Serve with broccoli.

Serves 4

300g sweet potatoes, cubed
2 carrots, cubed
1 cauliflower, in florets
400g extra lean minced beef
1 onion, chopped finely
1 courgette, chopped finely
100g fine green beans, chopped
100g mushrooms, sliced
1 tsp dried mixed herbs
4 tsp gravy granules for beef
steamed broccoli to serve.

one pot CHICKEN PILAU

  *per serving*

Preheat the oven to 180°C, Gas Mark 4. Mist a casserole with the cooking spray and fry the onion for 3 mins. Add the courgettes and pepper and cook for 2 mins. Meanwhile combine spices with some lemon zest and add half the mixture to the casserole along with the bay leaves, cloves and rice. Cook for 1 min, stirring. Tip the chickpeas into the casserole and add a squeeze of lemon juice. Bring to the boil, stir, cover and then bake in the oven for 20 mins.

Meanwhile, rub the reserved spice mix into the chicken breast and drizzle with lemon juice. Once the 20 mins are up, pop the chicken breasts on top of the rice, cover and put back in the oven for 25 mins. Remove the cloves and the bay leaves and serve with the yogurt and some steamed green veg.

Serves 4

*calorie controlled
  cooking spray
1 onion, chopped
2 courgettes, chopped
1 red pepper, chopped
2 tsp ground cumin
2 tsp ground coriander
½ tsp ground turmeric
1 lemon
2 bay leaves
6 whole cloves
175g dried brown rice
200g canned chickpeas,
  rinsed and drained
450ml chicken stock
4 x 150g skinless chicken
  breast fillets, slashed*

TO SERVE
*4 tbsp 0% fat natural
  Greek yogurt mixed
  with 3 tbsp chopped
  fresh coriander
steamed green veg*

PORK AND APRICOT

burgers

WITH SWEET POTATO CHIPS

 per serving

Serves 2

Preheat the oven to Gas Mark 6/200°C/fan oven 180°C. Lay the sweet potato wedges on a large baking tray lined with non-stick baking parchment. Mist with the cooking spray, sprinkle with sea salt and roast for 30 mins, turning once, until soft and golden.

Meanwhile, put the mince in a large bowl and combine with the apricots, thyme and pine nuts. Season well, then shape into 2 patties. Mist a non-stick frying or griddle pan with cooking spray and heat until hot. Cook the burgers for 8–10 mins, turning once, until cooked through and golden. Place a burger in each of the soft rolls along with a dollop of yogurt, some salad leaves and tomato slices. Serve with the sweet potato chips on the side.

1 sweet potato (300g), cut into wedges
calorie controlled cooking spray
sea salt
125g extra lean pork mince
35g ready-to-eat dried apricots,chopped finely
2 tsp chopped fresh thyme
15g toasted pine nuts, chopped roughly
salt and freshly ground black pepper

TO SERVE
2 medium soft brown rolls (50g each), toasted lightly
1 tbsp 0% fat natural Greek yogurt
fresh salad leaves and slices of tomato

From our gorgeous cookbook – Losing Weight the Smart Way*

* Available to buy in your meeting or our online shop.

SMART
snacking

Some people say never, ever, ever, eat between meals. We say, live your life, and if you want a snack, have a snack.

If you're in the zone, have a smart snack – we've got some awesomely good ideas for you here. But if it's got to be a bar of chocolate or a packet of crisps – eat it, track it, enjoy it.

WHAT ARE YOU REALLY HUNGRY FOR? HAVE A LOOK AT SMILE PAGE 24. IT MIGHT JUST SURPRISE YOU.

SAVOURY *snack attack*

cheese triangle with grapes

1 SmartPoints value

rice cake with 1 tsp smooth peanut butter

3 SmartPoints value

fat free tomato salsa & veg crudité

0 SmartPoints value

crumpet with 1 tsp marmite

4 SmartPoints value

1 hard boiled egg with baby spinach

2 SmartPoints value

3 seafood sticks & 1 tsp sweet chilli sauce

3 SmartPoints value

10 olives in brine

1 SmartPoints value

20g bag Lightly Sea Salted ProperCorn

3 SmartPoints value

46g wafer thin ham with pickled beetroot

1 SmartPoints value

1 tbsp guacamole & 2 extra thin crispbreads

2 SmartPoints value

1 tbsp reduced fat houmous & 2 extra thin crispbreads

3 SmartPoints value

pear & 20g reduced fat Cheddar cheese

2 SmartPoints value

SMART KALE CRISPS *per serving*

Serves 2

Preheat the oven to 190°C, Gas Mark 5. Wash the kale, pick the leaves (discard stalks) and dry very thoroughly. Put in a bowl with ½ tsp olive oil and toss well to coat. Lay the kale onto a non-stick baking sheet in a single layer (no overlapping, do in batches if needed). Bake for 15-20 mins, rotating the baking sheet half way. Remove from the oven when the crisps are crisp, but watch carefully, don't let them scorch (burnt kale crisps taste horrid!). Let the tray rest for 3 mins (they crisp up more), add salt and tuck in.

1 bag of kale
½ tsp olive oil

SMART LETTUCE WRAPS *per serving*

Serves 2

Top each lettuce leaf with ¼ of the ham/chicken/turkey, then with houmous and paprika. Cover with another lettuce leaf. Roll it up and tuck in.

8 leaves iceberg lettuce
30g wafer thin ham,
* chicken or turkey*
1 tbsp houmous
any herbs and veg
pinch of paprika

Sweet treats

2 squares any chocolate

4 SmartPoints value

Weight Watchers Yogurt

2 SmartPoints value

1 rich tea biscuit

1 SmartPoints value

1 chocolate digestive

4 SmartPoints value

1 Jaffa cake

2 SmartPoints value

Weight Watchers Rich Toffee Bar

3 SmartPoints value

½ papaya filled with raspberries

0 SmartPoints value

strawberries with balsamic vinegar

0 SmartPoints value

pot sugar-free ready to eat jelly

0 SmartPoints value

pot low-fat ready to eat custard with banana

5 SmartPoints value

60g sorbet

3 SmartPoints value

berries with 75g fat free fruit yogurt

2 SmartPoints value

SWEET *endings*

A little bit of what you fancy does you good. In fact, it's often when you stop yourself having a little bit of what you fancy, that you end up having way too much of what you fancy.

We've got some smart sweet ideas for you here – including some zero SmartPoints options – so it's easy to work these into your budget.

GORGEOUS *figs*

   per serving

Preheat the grill. Make a deep cross in the top of each fig and open them up like flowers. Put the figs on a baking tray and dust with icing sugar and a pinch of cinnamon. Cook for 5 mins making sure they don't burn. Serve in bowls with a dash of rosewater on each and a spoonful of yogurt.

 Leave out the icing sugar.

Serves 4

8 ripe figs
2 tsp icing sugar
pinch cinnamon
dash of rosewater
*4 tbsp 0% fat natural
  Greek yogurt*

SWEET
meringues

BASIC MERINGUE RECIPE *each*

Makes 16

Preheat the oven to 150°C, Gas Mark 2. Line a baking sheet with greaseproof paper and mist with calorie controlled cooking spray. Whisk egg whites, cream of tarter and salt in a clean bowl until foamy. Add Splenda a spoon at a time, whisking until stiff and glossy. Fold in vanilla. Spoon the meringue onto the baking sheet, trying to make each dollop even. (You can pipe into nests if you like). Bake for 18-20 mins.

calorie controlled
cooking spray
2 egg whites
¼ tsp cream of tarter
⅛ tsp salt
100g Splenda sugar
substitute
½ tsp vanilla extract

ETON MESS

Mix together 1 meringue nest (from recipe above) broken into small pieces, 3 tbsp 0% fat natural Greek yogurt and a handful of berries. **(Serves 1)**

FRUIT SALAD & QUARK MESS

Make a fruit salad (berries, sliced banana, orange segments and sliced kiwi are nice here), add 2 tbsp Quark and crumble over 1 meringue nest (from recipe above). **(Serves 1)**

POACHED *pear* WITH ALMONDS

   *per serving*

Place the pears in a pan, cover with water and poach gently for 8-10 mins or until tender, then drain.

Put 2 pear halves in each bowl, top with 4 roughly chopped almonds, drizzle with 1 tsp maple syrup and serve with 1 tbsp fromage frais.

Serves 4

4 ripe pears, peeled cored and halved
4 tsp maple syrup
16 whole almonds, roasted
4 tbsp fat free natural fromage frais

bubbly JELLIES

   *per serving*

Serves 4

Tip the contents of the jelly sachet into a bowl and pour the boiling water over, stir well to dissolve. Add the lemon juice, cool and chill in the fridge for 1 hour or until the jelly is almost ready to set (it will start to look thicker).

Gently mix together the berries and mint and divide between 4 glasses. Slowly mix the lemonade into the almost-set jelly then pour over the berries in the glasses. Cover with cling film and chill in the fridge for 2 hours or until set.

1 sachet sugar-free lemon & lime jelly
250ml boiling water
juice of 1 lemon
150g raspberries
100g blueberries
2 tsp chopped fresh mint
300ml diet lemonade

Grilled FRUIT

Grilling brings out the natural sweetness in fruit – **it's the perfect smart pudd.** Here are a few of our favourite combos but mix it up with whatever's in season.

 PEACHES OR NECTARINES

Halve and grill 1 peach (or nectarine) for 2-3 mins each side until caramelised. Serve with balsamic vinegar and chopped chilli with 1 tbsp of 0% fat natural yogurt, 1 tsp of runny honey and 1 grating of orange zest on each serving. **(Serves 1)**

 PINEAPPLE

Rub pineapple wedges with ground cinnamon and leave to infuse for 20 mins then grill until nicely charred. Top each portion with 1 (50g) scoop of low fat frozen yogurt. **(Serves 1)**

 BANANA *per serving*

Peel 2 ripe bananas and slice at an angle into 2cm slices. Grill for 2-3 mins each side until charred. Meanwhile peel back the lid from a 150g pot of low fat custard, push 2 squares of dark chocolate into the pot, re-cover and microwave on high for 1 min. Leave to stand for 1 min, stir and then divide into 2 small bowls and top with the bananas. **(Serves 2)**

 APPLE

Peel and core an apple and slice into 1cm thick slices. Grill over a medium heat until charred. Drizzle with 1 tsp maple syrup and 2 tsp toasted pecan nuts, crushed. **(Serves 1)**

FLAVOUR *boosters*

ZERO *heroes*

0 SmartPoints value™

MAKE YOUR MEALS COME ALIVE WITH THESE CONDIMENTS AND SEASONINGS.

1 tsp capers

chilli (fresh, dried or flakes)

1 tsp fat free tomato salsa

1 tbsp fish sauce (Nam Pla)

garlic

ginger

1 tsp harissa paste

herbs & spices (fresh or dried)

1 tsp hot pepper sauce (Tabasco)

lemongrass

lemon or lime juice

1 tsp mustard (any)

1 tsp soy sauce

1 tsp tomato purée

1 tbsp unsweetened pickled veg

1 tsp vanilla extract

vinegar

1 tsp Worcestershire sauce

1 tsp yeast extract (Marmite)

1 tsp zest of lemon, lime or orange

THE *special* ONES

1 SmartPoints value ™

GET A WHOLE LOAD OF ZING FOR 1 SMARTPOINTS VALUE.

SAVOURY

½ tsp toasted sesame oil

1 tsp grated parmesan

10 olives

SWEET

1 tsp mango chutney

1 tsp maple syrup

1 tsp chocolate sauce

CREAMY

10g feta cheese

1 tsp sour cream

1 tbsp mashed avocado

CRUNCHY

5g sunflower seeds

5 pistachios

5g slivered almonds

THE *lists*

SMARTPOINTS *food lists*

A

○ **Aduki beans**, cooked, 1 heaped tbsp, 35g	**1**
Alcohol	
See page 109 for the SmartPoints of a range of alcoholic drinks	
Almonds, 6, 13g	**2**
Anchovies, in oil, drained, 5, 15g	**1**
○ **Apple**	**0**
Apple juice, 1 medium glass, 250ml	**6**
Apple sauce, 1 tbsp, 20g	**1**
○ **Apricots, fresh or tinned in juice**, drained	**0**
Apricots, ready to eat, dried, 1 small pack, 50g	**4**
Apricots in juice, not drained, 1 large can, 410g	**9**
○ **Artichoke**	**0**
Artificial sweetener	**0**
○ **Asparagus**	**0**
○ **Aubergine**	**0**
Avocado, ½ medium, 77.5g	**5**

B

○ **Baby corn**	**0**
Bacon, back, fat trimmed, raw, 1 medium rasher, 25g	**1**
Bacon, back, raw, 1 rasher, 35g	**2**
○ **Bacon, medallions**, raw 2, 40g	**1**
Bacon, streaky, raw, 1 rasher, 20g	**2**
Bagel, 1 individual, 80g	**6**
○ **Baked beans**, 3 tbsp, 105g	**3**
○ **Baked beans, reduced sugar and salt**, 1 small can, 220g	**5**
Baking powder, 1 tbsp, 12g	**1**
○ **Banana**	**0**
Barbecue sauce, 2 tbsp, 30g,	**2**
○ **Beans, green**	**0**
○ **Beansprouts**	**0**
○ **Beef, braising steak, lean**, raw, 125g	**3**
Beef brisket, raw, 125g	**8**
Beef, burger, raw, 1 individual, 56g	**6**
○ **Beef, fillet steak, lean**, raw, 1 medium, 150g	**4**
Beef, fillet steak, raw, 1 medium, 150g	**6**
○ **Beef, mince, 5% fat**, raw, 125g	**3**
Beef, mince, 10% fat, raw, 125g	**6**
Beef, mince, raw, 125g	**8**

○ **Beef, rump steak, lean**, raw, 1 medium, 225g	**5**
Beef, rump steak, raw, 1 medium, 225g	**10**
○ **Beef, sirloin, lean**, raw, 1 medium, 225g	**5**
○ **Beef, stewing steak, lean**, raw, 125g	**2**
○ **Beetroot**, cooked or pickled	**0**
Black pudding, dry fried, 1 medium slice, 30g	**3**
○ **Blackberries**	**0**
○ **Blackcurrants**	**0**
○ **Blueberries**	**0**
○ **Borlotti beans**, cooked, 1 heaped tbsp, 35g	**1**
Bran flakes, 1 medium bowl, 30g	**4**
Brazil nuts, 2 individual, 6g	**1**
Bread, brown or white, 1 medium slice, 35g	**2**
Bread, brown, gluten-free, 1 medium slice, 35g	**3**
○ **Bread, calorie-controlled, brown** , 1 slice, 22g	**1**
Bread, calorie-controlled, white, 1 slice, 22g	**1**
Bread, ciabatta, 1 medium slice, 40g	**3**
Bread, farmhouse white or wholemeal, sliced, 1 medium slice, 35g	**2**
Bread, granary, unsliced, 40g	**3**
Bread, granary, sliced, 1 medium slice, 35g	**3**
Bread, pitta; white or wholemeal, 1 medium, 60g	**4**
Bread, white, gluten-free, 1 medium slice, 35g	**3**
Bread roll, crusty, 1 medium, 65g	**5**
Bread roll, soft white or wholemeal, 1 medium, 60g	**4**
Bread roll, gluten-free, white, 1 medium, 80g	**5**
Bread roll, granary, 1 medium, 65g	**4**
Breadcrumbs, dried, 1 tbsp, 20g	**2**
Brie, 40g	**5**
○ **Broad beans**, boiled, 1 heaped tbsp, 50g	**1**
○ **Broccoli**	**0**
Brown sauce, 2 tbsp, 30g	**2**
○ **Brussels sprouts**	**0**
○ **Bulgur wheat**, dry, 1 medium portion, 60g	**5**
Butter, 1 tsp, 5g	**2**
Butter, half-fat, 1 tsp, 5g	**1**
○ **Butter beans**, cooked, 1 heaped tbsp, 35g	**1**
Buttermilk, ½ pint, 248ml	**4**
○ **Butternut squash**	**0**

C

○ **Cabbage**	**0**
Calorie controlled cooking spray, 4 sprays, 0.8ml	**0**

Camembert, 1 medium portion, 40g	**4**
○ Cannellini beans, cooked, 1 heaped tbsp, 35g	**1**
Capers in brine	**0**
○ Carrots	**0**
Cashew nuts, 10 individual, 10g	**2**
○ Cauliflower	**0**
○ Celeriac	**0**
○ Celery	**0**
Cheddar, 40g	**6**
Cheddar, half-fat, 40g	**3**
Cheese slice, 1, 20g	**2**
Cheese slice, low-fat, 1, 20g	**1**
Cheese, soft, low-fat, 50g	**2**
Cheese, soft, medium-fat, 50g	**3**
Cheese triangle, 1, 14g	**1**
Cheese triangle, low-fat, 2, 28g	**1**
○ Cherries	**0**
Chestnuts, 4, 40g	**2**
Chia seeds, 15g	**2**
○ Chicken, breast, skinless, grilled, 1 medium, 120g	**2**
○ Chicken, breast, skinless, raw, 1, 165g	**2**
○ Chicken, drumstick, skinless, cooked, 1, edible portion 47g	**1**
Chicken, drumstick, with skin, cooked, 1, edible portion 62g	**2**
Chicken leg quarter with skin, roasted, 190g	**12**
○ Chicken, leg, skinless, raw, 1, 135g	**7**
○ Chicken, mince, raw, 125g	**2**
Chicken thigh, skinless, boneless, raw, 1 individual, 85g	**4**
○ Chicken, roasted mixed meat, skinless, 40g	**1**
Chicken, roast, mixed meat with skin, 40g	**2**
○ Chicken, wafer-thin, 2 slices, 46g	**1**
Chicken, wing, with skin, cooked, 1, edible portion, 25g	**1**
○ Chickpeas, cooked, 1 heaped tbsp, 35g	**1**
○ Chickpeas, dry, 50g	**4**
○ Chicory	**0**
Chilli sauce, 2 tbsp, 30g	**1**
○ Chilli, fresh	**0**
○ Chinese leaves (amaranth leaves)	**0**
Chips, homemade, thick cut, fried, 150g	**8**
Chips, fried, shop bought, 1 large portion, 240g	**18**
Chips, microwave, 1 small box, 100g	**7**
Chips, thick-cut, low-fat, oven baked, 150g	**6**
Chips, thick-cut, oven baked, 150g	**9**
Chocolate nut spread, 1 heaped tsp, 7.5g	**2**
Chocolate, any type, 2 squares, 14g	**4**
Chocolate, any type, 1 bar, 45g	**12**
Chocolate mousse, low fat, 1 pot, 65g	**4**
Chorizo, 3 slices, 15g	**2**
○ Clams in brine, drained, 50g	**1**
○ Clementines	**0**
○ Cockles in vinegar, 1 jar, 155g, drained	**1**
○ Cockles, boiled, 1 portion, 110g	**1**

Cocoa powder, 1 heaped tsp, 6g	**1**
Coconut, creamed, 1 sachet, 50g	**18**
Coconut, fresh, 100g	**19**
Coconut milk, ¼ can, 100ml	**9**
Coconut milk, reduced-fat, ¼ can, 100ml	**4**
Coconut oil, 1 tsp, 5ml	**3**
Coconut water, 1 small carton, 330ml	**3**
○ Cod, unsmoked or smoked, raw, 1 fillet, 120g	**1**
Cola, 1 can, 330ml	**8**
Cola, diet	**0**
Coleslaw, 1 tbsp, 45g	**3**
Coleslaw, reduced-calorie, 1 tbsp, 40g	**2**
Corn flakes, 30g	**3**
○ Corn on the cob, 1 medium, 230g	**5**
Corned beef, 1 medium slice, 35g	**2**
Corn flour, 1 level tbsp, 20g	**2**
Cottage cheese, natural, 1 tbsp, 40g	**1**
○ Cottage cheese, natural, reduced-fat, 1 small tub, 150g	**3**
○ Courgette	**0**
Couscous, cooked, 150g	**7**
Couscous, white, dry, 60g	**6**
○ Couscous, wholewheat, dry, 60g	**6**
○ Crab, canned in brine, 1 small can, 85g	**1**
○ Crab, boiled, 1, 110g	**2**
Crab, dressed, 100g	**3**
○ Cranberries, fresh	**0**
Cranberry juice, 1 medium glass, 250ml	**7**
Cranberry sauce, 1 tbsp, 30g	**3**
○ Crayfish, raw, 85g	**1**
Cream, canned spray, 1 tbsp, 10g	**1**
Cream, clotted, 1 tbsp, 30g	**9**
Cream, double, 1 tbsp, 15ml	**4**
Cream, single, 1 tbsp, 15ml	**1**
Cream, whipping, 1 tbsp, 15ml	**3**
Cream cheese, 40g	**8**
Cream cracker, 1, 7g	**1**
Crème fraîche, 1 level tbsp, 30g	**6**
Crème fraîche, half-fat, 1 level tbsp, 30g	**2**
Crispbreads, extra-thin, 3, 15g	**1**
Crispbreads, 2, 10g	**1**
Croissant, 1, 60g	**8**
Croutons, 1 tbsp, 7g	**1**
○ Crumpets, 1, 60g	**4**
○ Cucumber	**0**
Currants, 1 heaped tbsp, 25g	**4**
Curry paste, 1 tsp, 15g	**1**
Curry powder, 1 tsp, 10g	**1**
Custard, ready to eat, 1 pot, 150g	**7**
Custard, ready to eat, low-fat, 1 pot, 150g	**5**
Custard cream, 1, 12g	**3**
Custard powder, 1 tbsp, 15g	**1**

D

○ Damson, fresh	0
Date, dried, 1, 15g	2
Digestive biscuit, 1, 13g	2
Digestive biscuit, chocolate, 1, 17g	4
○ Dover sole, 1, 250g	2
Drinking chocolate, 1 tbsp, 18g	4
Duck, breast, skinless, raw, 1 medium, 150g	4
Duck, breast, with skin, raw, 1 medium, 160g	10

E

Edam, 40g	5
○ Egg white	0
○ Egg whole, 1 medium, 52g	2
Egg yolk, 1 medium, 20g	2
○ Elderberries	0
Elderflower cordial, diluted, 1 glass, 250ml	4

F

○ Fennel	0
Feta, 40g	4
Feta, light, 40g	2
○ Fig	0
Filo Pastry, 1 large sheet, 45g	4
○ Flageolet beans, cooked, 1 heaped tbsp, 35g	1
Flour, any type, 1 level tbsp, 20g	2
Frankfurter, 1, 47g	5
○ Fresh fruit salad (no added sugar)	0
○ Fromage frais, natural, 1 tbsp, 45g	1
Fromage frais, fat-free, fruit, 1 medium tub, 100g	1
○ Fromage frais, fat-free, natural, 2 tbsp, 90g	1
Fromage frais, fruit flavoured, 1 small tub, 100g	4
Fromage frais, low fat, fruit, 1 tbsp, 45g	2
○ Fruit cocktail, in juice, drained	0
Fruit cocktail, in syrup, 1 small can, 210g	7

G

○ Gammon steak, raw, 1 average, 170g	5
○ Garlic	0
Gelatine, 2 sachets, 25g	1
Ghee, 1 level tsp, 5g	2
○ Gherkins	0
Ginger beer, 1 can, 330ml	6
○ Goat, raw, 100g	1
Goat's cheese, 40g	5
○ Gooseberries	0
○ Gourd (karela)	0
Grape juice, 1 medium glass, 250ml	9
○ Grapefruit	0
Grapefruit juice, 1 medium glass, 250ml	5
○ Grapefruit segments, in juice, drained	0
○ Grapes	0

Gravy granules, prepared, 60ml	1
Gravy granules, unprepared, 2 level tsp, 6g	1
○ Green beans	0
Guacamole, 1 tbsp, 30g	1
○ Guava	0

H

○ Haddock, unsmoked or smoked, raw, 1 fillet, 120g	1
Halloumi, 40g	5
Halloumi, light, 40g	3
○ Ham, premium, 1 slice, 35g	1
○ Ham, wafer-thin, 2 slices, 46g	1
Hazelnuts, 10, 10g	2
Herbs, dried	0
○ Herbs, fresh	0
Hoisin sauce, 1 tbsp, 15g	2
Honey, 1 heaped tsp, 8g	1
Horseradish sauce, 1 tbsp, 20g	1
Hot cross bun, 1 medium, 70g	8
Hot pepper sauce (Tabasco)	0
Houmous, 1 tbsp, 30g	3
Houmous, reduced-fat, 1 tbsp, 30g	2

I

Ice cream, premium dairy, 1 scoop, 60g	8
Ice cream, low-fat, 1 scoop, 60g	4
Ice cream, vanilla, 1 scoop, 60g	5

J

Jaffa Cake, 1, 12g	2
Jam, 1 heaped tsp, 18g	3
Jam, low calorie, 2 level tsp, 16g	1
Jelly made with water, 1 serving, 125g	4
Jelly, ready to eat, 1 pot, 125g	6
○ Jelly crystals, sugar-free, ¼ package, 3g	0
○ Jelly, sugar free, ready to eat, 1 small pot, 125g	0

K

○ Kale	0
○ Kidney beans, cooked, 1 heaped tbsp, 35g	1
○ Kidney beans, dried, 100g	6
○ King prawns, cooked, 8 shelled, 100g	1
○ King prawns, raw, 10 raw, 100g	1
Kipper, grilled, 1 fillet, 130g	8
○ Kiwi fruit	0

L

Lamb breast, roasted, 1 medium slice, 30g	4
Lamb, boneless leg steak, lean, raw, 1 average, 100g	5
Lamb, chump chop, boneless, raw, 1 average, 130g	10
Lamb, leg, roasted, 1 slice, 30g	2
Lamb, loin chop, raw, 1 average, 60g	6
Lamb, mince, lean, raw, 125g	7

Lamb, mince, raw, 125g	**10**
Lard, 1 tsp, 7g	**3**
○ Leek	**0**
○ Lemon	**0**
Lemon curd, 1 heaped tsp, 18g	**3**
Lemon juice, fresh	**0**
Lemonade, 1 can, 330ml	**5**
Lemonade, diet	**0**
○ Lentils, brown or green or red, cooked, 1 heaped tbsp, 35g	**1**
○ Lentils, brown or green, dry, 50g	**3**
○ Lentils, red, dry, 50g	**4**
○ Lettuce	**0**
○ Lime	**0**
○ Liver, calf or pig, raw 100g	**2**
○ Liver, chicken, raw, 100g	**1**
○ Liver, lamb, raw, 100g	**3**
○ Loganberries	**0**
○ Lychees	**0**
Lychees, in syrup, 2, 26g	**1**

M

Macadamia nuts, 5, 10g	**3**
Mackerel, in brine, 1 can, drained, 86g	**6**
Mackerel, in tomato sauce, 1 can, 125g	**7**
Mackerel, raw, 1 fillet, 150g	**10**
Mackerel, smoked, 1 fillet, 100g	**8**
Malt extract, 1 tbsp, 15g	**3**
Malt loaf, 1 small slice, 35g	**4**
○ Mandarin	**0**
○ Mandarin segments, in juice, drained	**0**
Mandarin segments, in syrup, 1 small can, 210g	**7**
○ Mango	**0**
Mango, in syrup, ½ can, 213g	**10**
Maple syrup, 1 tsp, 7g	**1**
Margarine, 1 tsp, 5g	**1**
Marmalade, 1 heaped tsp, 18g	**3**
Marmalade, reduced-sugar, 1 heaped tsp, 18g	**2**
○ Marrow	**0**
Mascarpone, 40g	**9**
Mayonnaise, 1 tsp, 5g	**1**
Mayonnaise, reduced-fat, 1 tbsp, 15g	**1**
Melba toast, 6 slices, 21g	**2**
○ Melon	**0**
Meringue nest, 1, 12g	**3**
Milk, semi-skimmed, 1 pint, 568ml	**11**
Milk, semi-skimmed, ½ pint, 284ml	**5**
Milk, semi-skimmed, ¼ pint, 142ml	**3**
○ Milk, skimmed, 1 pint, 568ml	**7**
○ Milk, skimmed, ½ pint, 284ml	**4**
○ Milk, skimmed, ¼ pint, 142ml	**2**
Milk, soya, sweetened, 1 pint, 568ml	**8**
Milk, soya, sweetened, ½ pint, 284ml	**4**
Milk, soya, sweetened, ¼ pint, 142ml	**2**

○ Milk, soya, unsweetened, 1 pint, 568ml	**4**
○ Milk, soya, unsweetened, ½ pint, 284ml	**2**
○ Milk, soya, unsweetened, ¼ pint, 142ml	**1**
Milk, whole, 1 pint, 568ml	**16**
Milk, whole, ½ pint, 284ml	**8**
Milk, whole, ¼ pint, 142ml	**4**
Mint jelly, 1 tbsp, 18g	**2**
Mint sauce, 2 tsp, 10g	**1**
○ Mixed beans, cooked, 1 heaped tbsp, 35g	**1**
Mozzarella, 40g	**4**
Mozzarella, light, 40g	**2**
Muesli, added sugar, 50g	**7**
Muesli, no sugar or salt, 50g	**6**
Muffin, English, white, 1, 70g	**5**
Muffin, English, wholemeal, 1, 70g	**5**
○ Mung beans, cooked, 1 heaped tbsp, 35g	**1**
○ Mung beans, dried, 50g	**3**
○ Mushrooms	**0**
○ Mussels, boiled, no shells, 40g	**1**
○ Mussels, weighed with shells, 120g	**1**
Mustard, coarse grain, 1 heaped tsp, 15g	**1**
Mustard, Dijon, 1 level tbsp, 15g	**1**
○ Mustard cress	**0**

n

Naan bread, ½ medium, 70g	**6**
○ Nectarine	**0**
Noodles, egg, boiled, 150g	**7**
Noodles, egg, dry, 60g	**6**

O

Oatcakes, 1, 13g	**2**
○ Oats, 30g	**3**
Oil, any type, 1 tsp, 5ml	**2**
○ Okra	**0**
Olives, in brine, 10, 30g	**1**
○ Onion	**0**
○ Orange	**0**
Orange juice, concentrate, unsweetened, 50ml	**5**
Orange juice, unsweetened, 250ml	**5**
○ Oysters, raw, 12, 120g	**1**

P

Paneer, 40g	**5**
○ Papaya (pawpaw)	**0**
Parma ham, 1 thin slice, 17g	**1**
Parmesan, 1 tbsp, 15g	**2**
○ Parsnip, 1 medium, 90g	**2**
○ Passata	**0**
○ Passion fruit	**0**
Pasta, corn, dry, 40g	**3**
Pasta, fresh, cooked, 140g	**6**
Pasta, fresh, raw, 80g	**6**
Pasta, white, dry, 60g	**6**

○ **Pasta, wholewheat**, dry, 60g	**6**
Pastry, puff, 50g	**7**
Pastry, short crust, ready rolled, uncooked, 50g	**8**
○ **Peach**	**0**
Peaches, dried, 25g	**3**
○ **Peaches, in juice, drained**	**0**
Peanut butter, crunchy or smooth, 15g	**3**
Peanut butter, reduced-fat, 15g	**3**
Peanuts, plain, unsalted, 25g	**4**
○ **Pear**	**0**
Pearl barley, dry, 30g	**3**
○ **Pears, in juice, drained**	**0**
○ **Peas**, 80g	**2**
Pecan nuts, 3, 18g	**4**
○ **Peppers**	**0**
Pesto sauce, 1 level tbsp, 15g	**2**
○ **Physalis (cape gooseberry)**	**0**
○ **Pickled onions**	**0**
Pilchards, in brine, 1 small can, drained, 116g	**5**
Pilchards, in tomato sauce, 1 small can, 105g	**3**
Pine nuts, 50g	**11**
○ **Pineapple**	**0**
○ **Pineapple, in juice, drained**	**0**
Pineapple juice, 250ml	**6**
○ **Pinto beans**, cooked, 1 heaped tbsp, 35g	**1**
Pistachios, 15, 15g	**3**
Pizza base, thin & crispy, 9 inch, 120g	**10**
Pizza base mix, ¼ pack, 35g	**3**
○ **Plaice**, raw, 1 fillet, 130g	**1**
○ **Plantain**, cooked, 1 medium, 180g	**7**
○ **Plums**	**0**
Polenta, dry, 1 medium, 60g	**6**
○ **Pomegranate**	**0**
○ **Popcorn, plain or salted (no added oil or flavours)**, 25g	**3**
Popcorn, popped with oil, 25g	**4**
Popcorn, sweet, 25g	**4**
○ **Popping corn**, uncooked, 50g	**5**
○ **Pork, escalope**, raw, 1 average, 130g	**3**
○ **Pork, fillet, lean**, raw, 100g	**3**
Pork mince, lean, raw, 125g	**5**
○ **Pork, loin steak, lean**, raw, 1 average, 150g	**6**
○ **Pork, mince, extra-lean**, raw, 125g	**3**
○ **Pork, tenderloin**, raw, 150g	**3**
Potato salad, 125g	**6**
○ **Potatoes**, raw, 200g	**5**
○ **Prawns**, peeled & cooked, 100g	**1**
Prunes, 50g	**4**
Prunes in juice, 1 small can, 210g	**10**
Prunes in syrup, 1 small can, 210g	**11**
○ **Puffed wheat, no added sugar or salt**, 20g	**2**
○ **Pumpkin**	**0**
Pumpernickel bread, 1 medium slice, 26g	**2**
Pumpkin seeds, 1 tbsp, 10g	**2**

Q

○ **Quark**, 1 heaped tbsp, 55g	**1**
○ **Quinoa**, dry, 1 medium portion, 60g	**5**
○ **Quorn fillet**, 1, 51g	**1**
○ **Quorn, mince**, 100g	**2**
○ **Quorn, pieces**, 75g	**1**
Quorn, sausage, 1, 50g	**1**

R

○ **Radish**	**0**
Raisins, 1 heaped tbsp, 30g	**5**
○ **Raspberries**	**0**
○ **Raspberries, in juice, drained**	**0**
Raspberries, in syrup, 1 small can, 210g	**11**
Redcurrant jelly, 2 tsp, 10g	**1**
○ **Redcurrants**	**0**
○ **Rhubarb**	**0**
Rhubarb in syrup, 150g	**3**
Rice cakes, 3, 21g	**2**
Rice crispies, 30g	**4**
Rice pudding, ½ large can, 200g	**7**
Rice pudding, low-fat, ½ can, 200g	**7**
○ **Rice, brown**, dry, 60g	**6**
Rice, white long grain, dry, 60g	**6**
Rich tea biscuit, 1, 7g	**1**
Ricotta, 40g	**2**
○ **Rocket**	**0**

S

Salad cream, 1 tbsp, 15g	**2**
Salad cream, light, 1 tbsp, 15g	**1**
Salad dressing, blue cheese, 1 tbsp, 15ml	**2**
Salad dressing, Caesar, 1 tbsp, 15ml	**3**
Salad dressing, Caesar, low-fat, 1 tbsp, 15ml	**1**
Salad dressing, French, 1 tbsp, 15ml	**2**
Salad dressing, Italian, 1 tbsp, 15ml	**4**
Salad dressing, low-fat, 2 tbsp, 30ml	**1**
Salad dressing, fat free, 2 tbsp, 30ml	**1**
Salad dressing, Thousand Island, 1 tbsp, 30g	**3**
Salad dressing, Thousand Island, reduced-fat, 1 tbsp, 30g	**1**
Salami, 1 large slice, 11g	**2**
○ **Salmon, canned, pink**, ½ large can, 107g	**2**
○ **Salmon**, raw, 1 fillet, 130g	**5**
Salmon, smoked, 60g	**2**
Sardines, in brine, 1 small can, drained, 86g	**3**
Sardines, in tomato sauce, 1 small can, 120g	**5**
○ **Sardines**, raw, 1, 60g	**2**
○ **Satsumas**	**0**
Sausages, beef, raw, 1, 57g	**5**
Sausages, pork, raw, 1, 20g	**2**
Sausages, vegetarian, 1, 50g	**2**

○ **Scallops**, steamed, 9 small, 54g	**1**
Scone, fruit or plain, 1, 60g	**8**
○ **Seafood selection**, 100g	**1**
○ **Seafood sticks**, 2, 31g	**1**
Sesame seeds, 1 tbsp, 12g	**2**
○ **Shallots**	**0**
○ **Sharon fruit (persimmon)**	**0**
Shortbread, 1, 20g	**4**
○ **Shrimps**, 100g	**1**
Soy sauce, 1, 5ml	**0**
○ **Soya beans**, cooked, 1 heaped tbsp, 35g	**1**
Spaghetti, canned in tomato sauce, 1 small can, 200g	**5**
Spices	**0**
○ **Spinach**	**0**
Spread, low-fat, 1 level tsp, 5g	**1**
Spread, soya, 1 tsp, 5g	**1**
Spread, very low-fat, 2 tsp, 10g	**1**
○ **Spring onions**	**0**
○ **Squid**, raw, 60g	**1**
Stilton, 40g	**7**
Stock cubes, any type, 1, 10g	**1**
Stock gel, 1 unprepared, 28g	**2**
○ **Strawberries**	**0**
Strawberries in syrup, 1 small can, 200g	**8**
Sugar, 1 tsp, 5g	**1**
Sugar, Demerara, 100g	**25**
○ **Sugar snap peas**	**0**
Sultanas, 1 heaped tbsp, 30g	**5**
Sun-dried tomatoes, 25g	**2**
Sun-dried tomatoes in oil, 25g	**2**
Sunflower seeds, 1 tbsp, 10g	**2**
○ **Swede**	**0**
Sweet chilli sauce, 1 tsp, 5g	**1**
○ **Sweet potato**, raw, 150g	**5**
○ **Sweetcorn**, 1 tbsp, 30g	**1**
○ **Sweetcorn, baby**	**0**

T

○ **Tangerines**	**0**
Taramasalata, 1 tbsp, 30g	**5**
Tartare sauce, 1 tbsp, 15g	**2**
Teriyaki sauce, 2 level tsp, 10g	**1**
Thai fish sauce, 1 tbsp, 30g	**1**
○ **Tofu, regular or smoked**, 50g	**1**
○ **Tomato, fresh or tinned**	**0**
Tomato juice, 250ml	**2**
Tomato ketchup, 2 tbsp, 30g	**2**
Tomato purée, 1 serving, 20g	**1**
Tonic water, 1 mini bottle/can, 150ml	**2**
Tonic water, low-calorie	**0**
Tortilla wrap, 1, 42g	**4**
○ **Trout**, raw, 1 fillet, 120g	**3**
○ **Tuna, in brine or spring water**, drained, 70g	**1**
Tuna, in oil, drained, 70g	**2**

○ **Tuna**, raw, 1 steak, 140g	**2**
○ **Turkey, breast mince**, raw, 125g	**2**
○ **Turkey, breast, skinless**, raw, 125g	**1**
Turkey, mince, raw, 125g	**3**
○ **Turkey, rasher**, grilled, 2 rashers, 66g	**1**
○ **Turkey, roasted, skinless**, 1 slice, 30g	**1**
○ **Turkey, steak**, raw, 1 average, 150g	**1**
○ **Turkey thigh**, raw, 125g	**2**
○ **Turkey, wafer-thin**, 46g	**1**
○ **Turnip**	**0**
Tzatziki, 1 tbsp, 30g	**1**

V

○ **Venison, lean**, raw, 125g	**1**
Vinegar, all types, 1 tbsp, 15ml	**0**

W

Walnut halves, 3, 9g	**2**
Water biscuit, 1, 8g	**1**
○ **Water chestnuts**	**0**
○ **Watercress**	**0**
Whitebait, fried, 80g	**11**
Weetabix, 1 biscuit, 19g	**2**
○ **Wholegrain wheat cereal, (Shredded Wheat)**, 2 biscuits, 45g	**4**
Worcestershire sauce	**0**

Y

○ **Yam**, 150g	**5**
Yeast extract	**0**
Yogurt, fat-free, fruit, 1 pot, 150g	**4**
○ **Yogurt, fat-free, natural**, 1 pot, 150g	**3**
Yogurt, Greek, natural, 1 pot, 150g	**9**
○ **Yogurt, Greek, natural, 0% fat**, 1 pot, 150g	**2**
Yogurt, low-fat, fruit, 1 pot, 150g	**6**
○ **Yogurt, low-fat, natural**, 1 pot, 150g	**4**
Yogurt, low fat plain, frozen, 100g	**3**
Yogurt, soya, fruit flavoured, 125g	**4**
○ **Yogurt, soya, plain**, 1 pot, 150g	**2**
Yorkshire pudding, 1, 20g	**1**

Alcohol

Please note – you can't calculate the SmartPoints of alcohol using the nutritional information. To help you, here's a list of some popular alcoholic drinks. Search the digital tools for more.

Beer, bitter, average, 1 pint, 568ml	**7**
Beer, bitter, average, 1 can, 440ml	**6**
Brandy, 1 single measure, 25ml	**2**
Champagne, 1 flute, 125ml	**4**
Champagne, 1 bottle, 750ml	**21**
Cider, dry, 1 pint, 568ml	**9**
Cider, low-alcohol, 1 bottle, 500ml	**5**
Cider, sweet, 1 pint, 568ml	**11**
Cream liqueurs, 1 single measure, 25ml	**4**
Gin, 1 single measure, 25ml	**2**
Lager, l pint, 568ml	**5**
Lager, alcohol-free, 1 pint, 568ml	**2**
Lager, low-alcohol, 1 bottle, 330ml	**2**
Pimms, 1 single measure, 25ml	**2**
Pimms, 1 double measure, 50ml	**3**
Port, 1 double measure, 50ml	**3**
Rum, 1 single measure, 25ml	**2**
Schnapps, fruit flavour, 1 single measure, 25ml	**2**
Sherry, dry or medium, 1 double measure, 50ml	**2**
Sherry, sweet, 1 double measure, 50ml	**3**
Tequila, 1 single measure, 25ml	**2**
Vodka, 1 single measure, 25ml	**2**
Whisky/bourbon, 1 single measure, 25ml	**2**
Wine, low alcohol, (6% vol), 1 medium glass, 175ml	**3**
Wine, red, 1 medium glass, 175ml	**4**
Wine, rosé or sparkling, 1 medium glass, 175ml	**5**
Wine, white, dry or medium, 1 medium glass, 175ml	**5**
Wine, white, sweet, 1 medium glass, 175ml	**7**

To avoid risks to health, women are advised to drink no more than 2-3 units of alcohol a day (3-4 units for men) and everyone should aim for at least 2 alcohol-free days a week.

SMARTPOINTS FOR FRUITS AND VEGETABLES

Whilst most fruits and vegetables are zero SmartPoints – there are a few exceptions, as listed below. If in doubt, check the Food Lists or the digital tools*.

- Avocado
- Cassava/yucca/manioc
- Fruit canned in natural juice, not drained
- Fruit canned in syrup
- Dried fruit, including prunes
- Olives
- Parsnips
- Peas (except sugar snap/ snow peas/mange tout)
- Plantain
- Potato, including sweet potato

LOOK OUT FOR SHOP**

The directory for supermarket shopping – SmartPoints for thousands of foods and drinks including your favourite supermarkets and brands.

* For Subscribers.
** Available to buy in your meeting or our online shop.

THE NO COUNT food list

Bacon medallions

Baked beans

BEANS & PULSES
Aduki
Black-eyed
Borlotti
Broad
Butter
Cannellini
Chick peas
Flageolet
French
Green
Haricot
Kidney
Lentils
Mixed pulses
Mung
Pinto
Runner
Soya
Split peas

BEEF
Braising steak, lean
Fillet steak, lean
Mince, extra lean (5% fat)
Rump steak, lean
Silverside, lean
Sirloin steak, lean
Stewing steak, lean

Bread, brown
 calorie controlled
Buckwheat
Bulgur wheat

CHEESE
Cottage cheese,
 reduced fat,
 natural
Quark

CHICKEN
Breast, skinless
Drumstick, skinless
Leg, skinless
Mince
Wafer thin

Couscous, wholewheat
Crumpets

EGGS
Egg White
Duck
Goose
Hen
Quail

FISH*
Cod
Cod, smoked
Coley
Dover sole
Grouper
Haddock
Haddock, smoked
Hake
Halibut
Herring roe, soft
Hoki
John Dory
Lemon sole

Monkfish
Mullet
Orange roughy
Pike
Plaice
Pollock
Red snapper
Rock salmon
Salmon
Salmon, tinned, pink/red
Sardines
Sea bass
Sea bream (red fish)
Shark
Skate
Squid
Swordfish
Tilapia
Trout
Trout, smoked
Tuna
Tuna in brine/
 spring water
Turbot
Whiting

Fromage frais,
 natural, fat free

FRUIT
Fresh (except avocado)
Frozen
Tinned in natural
 juice, drained

Gammon steak,
 lean

Garlic

Ginger

Goat

Guinea Fowl

HAM
Premium
Pre-packed slices
Wafer thin

Heart, lamb's
Herbs, fresh

Jelly, sugar free

KIDNEY
Lamb
Pig

LIVER
Calf
Chicken
Lamb
Ox
Pig

MEAT FREE
Bacon style rashers
Fillets
Mince
Pieces
Soya mince
Tofu, regular/smoked

MILK
Skimmed
Unsweetened almond
Unsweetened soya

Millet

Nori

Oat bran
Oats
Octopus

Partridge
Passata
Pasta, wholewheat
Pigeon

Popping corn kernels

PORK
Escalope
Fillet, lean
Leg, lean
Loin steak, lean
Mince, extra lean (5% fat)
Shoulder, lean
Tenderloin

POTATOES
All types

Puffed wheat, no added
    sugar or salt

Quail
Quinoa

Rabbit

RICE
Brown
Wild

Sandwich thins, brown
Seafood sticks

SHELLFISH
Clams
Cockles
Crab
Crab, in brine, drained
Crayfish
Lobster
Mussels
Oysters
Prawns, all types
Scallops
Shrimps
Whelks
Winkles

TURKEY
Breast mince
Breast, skinless
Roasted, skinless
Steak
Thigh, skinless

Wafer thin

Veal escalope

VEGETABLES
Fresh
Frozen
Tinned in water

Venison, lean

Wheat bran
Wheat germ
Wholegrain wheat
    cereal (similar to
    Shredded Wheat)

Yam

YOGURT
Fat-free, natural
Greek, 0% fat natural
Low-fat, natural
Soya, plain

**WEIGHT WATCHERS
PRODUCTS**
Extra Trimmed
    Unsmoked Back
    Bacon
Original Breakfast Oats
Petits Pains
Pitta Bread
Quark
Sliced Brown Danish Bread
Tortillas
Wraps

FOR BRANDED NO COUNT FOODS CHECK OUT THE WEIGHT WATCHERS APP OR SHOP GUIDE.

wellbeing

NURSING MUMS

Health professionals recommend that babies are exclusively breastfed for the first six months and that breast milk continues to be an important part of a baby's diet for the first year of life*.

Whilst breastfeeding, SmartPoints is designed to lead to a weight loss of up to 1lb a week. Losing more weight than this may affect the quality and quantity of your breast milk. Your Leader will check your daily SmartPoints allowance, and then you will need to:

Add 16 SmartPoints values to your daily allowance if breast milk is the sole source of nutrition for your baby, and don't drop below 52 SmartPoints values a day. If you are weaning your baby and supplementing breastfeeding with solid foods, add 6 SmartPoints values to your daily allowance. If you're using the No Count approach, continue to use the No Count foods list with no change to your weekly SmartPoints allowance.

Speak to your Health Visitor for more information about following a healthy diet while breastfeeding.

TYPE 2 DIABETES

Weight Watchers offers members with type 2 diabetes a safe weight-loss approach that promotes healthy living and can help effectively control the condition for life.

We recommend that you share your weight-loss plan with your diabetic health professional. Any recommendations that are provided by a qualified health professional should supersede anything you receive as part of your Weight Watchers membership.

MENOPAUSE

Menopause and the treatment for it (HRT) are often blamed for causing weight gain. However, there is currently no conclusive evidence that they are directly linked with a gain in weight. More directly linked with weight gain is the ageing process itself, as you need less energy to maintain a healthy weight.

Our approach accounts for this by taking your age into consideration when calculating your SmartPoints budget. Weight loss can help ease the symptoms of the menopause. By following the SmartPoints approach you can regain control of your weight.

For in-depth information on these conditions and weight loss, go to weightwatchers.co.uk/wellbeing or speak to your leader.

*Department of Health, Infant Feeding Recommendation, 2003, Crown.

Thermal Physics